INDEX

ON CENSORSHIP

GÖRAN OLLSEN

Chechnya 1995

INDEX ON CENSORSHIP 2 1995

Volume 24 No 2 March/April 1995   Issue 163

Index on Censorship (ISSN 0306-4220) is published
bimonthly by a non-profit-making company: Writers &
Scholars International Ltd, Lancaster House,
33 Islington High Street, London N1 9LH
Tel: 0171-278 2313 Fax: 0171-278 1878
E-mail: indexoncenso@gn.apc.org
Internet Gopher site: mary.iia.org 70

Index on Censorship is associated with Writers &
Scholars Educational Trust, registered charity
number 325003

Second class postage (US subscribers only) paid at
Irvington, New Jersey. Postmaster: send US address
changes to Index on Censorship c/o Virgin Mailing &
Distribution, 10 Camptown Road, Irvington, NJ 07111

Subscriptions 1995 (6 issues p.a.): £32 (overseas £38
or US$48). Students £24/US$36

Former Editors: Michael Scammell (1972-81); Hugh Lunghi (1981-83); George Theiner (1983-88); Sally Laird (1988-89); Andrew Graham-Yooll (1989-93)

EDITORIAL

Possible expectations

In the bad old days, dissident Soviet writers used to say that what they needed from the West was not just admiration for their courage in challenging what made them unfree, but a sense that we too were busy, in our own world, at the work of freedom.

It cannot be said that in Britain the matter of free expression has been high on the list of priorities. We still have no Bill of Rights, no written constitution, no Freedom of Information Act: we have reduced people's rights to protest; allowed media ownership to concentrate in ever fewer hands, thus restricting diversity and choice; seen whistleblowers punished for defending the public interest. Much of this seems to be a matter of indifference. There is, if anything, a desire for more social controls.

Looking at *Index*'s daily in-tray with its countless tales of atrocities committed round the world in the name of censorship, it is hard not to think that we are what Ted Hughes once described as 'the spoilt brats of Western civilisation, disappointed of impossible expectations and deprived of the revelations of necessity.' Freedom may itself be indivisible, but we live in various states of liberty. We in Britain may not live under despots, but unless we cultivate and defend those liberties we already have, we will become ever more a society that prefers the keepers of secrets to the tellers of tales.

America's national discourse has shifted so dramatically that events that would once have roused the liberal conscience hardly rate a mention. This issue of *Index* looks at the death penalty in the USA, 20 years ago on the retreat, now a vote winner for Democrats as well as Republicans and returning even to the most liberal states. By the time you read this, Mumia Abu-Jamal, a journalist, innocent of murder but on death row for 12 years, could have been executed.

Ariel Dorfman's powerful play, *Death and the Maiden*, first published in *Index* in 1991, is about atrocities in another time and another place. Now a film, directed by Roman Polanski, the proceeds from the London première on 19 April will go to *Index* (see inside front cover). ❏

Ursula Owen

C O N T E N T S

LETTERS

Rwanda 1994: what should we be doing?

A clarification

From Philip Johnston, president, CARE, USA

I would like to make the following observations on Alex de Waal's 'African Encounters' *(Index* November/December 1994).

Mr de Waal's opening contention that humanitarian organisations are calling for military intervention openly and frequently in ways unthinkable five years ago, uses Somalia as a case in point. Mr de Waal has not included data that you would want your readers to have.

Mr de Waal states: 'The agency most responsible for the call for US intervention was CARE-US.' What is not included is any reference to time or sequences of events. Permit me, therefore to clarify for your readers the issue of military intervention and who called for what to happen.

As early as mid-1992, the UN operation in Somalia (UNOSOM) had entered into discussions with UN-NY to bring into Somalia military troops that would be under the UN. The issue was debated within the UN Security Council, and it was finally decided, pending the agreement of member states, to provide the forces. In July or August 1992, the four defence areas were agreed to and the UN set about securing troops. Mr de Waal omits to mention the arrival of the first of the four units. Five hundred Pakistani soldiers arrived via US military transport in September. Military intervention based solely on UN assessments had begun long before the bulk of the NGOs arrived in Somalia.

A second omission is any mention of UNOSOM's role in securing a multinational military airlift of food from Mombasa, Kenya to locations in southern Somalia. The UN request was made to its members through the secretary general, and Canada, Belgium, the USA, and Germany took part. All of this was debated in the summer of 1992 and in place by September 1992, before most of the NGOs arrived in Somalia.

Mr de Waal does not give sufficient credit to the role of UNOSOM in recognising the deteriorating health conditions of Somalia and the worsening security conditions. Nor does he credit UNOSOM with seeking assistance from countries to deploy their military for humanitarian purposes.

Permit me to add one historical footnote. The military forces continued to carry food by plane from Mombasa until the roads and bridges were repaired, enabling the humanitarian community to transport food by road.

It is inaccurate to attribute the call for military intervention to any one NGO, or a collection of NGOs. The fact is that long before the American marines arrived in December 1992, UNOSOM's military advisors had convinced the UN and a number of its members to become engaged. The second observation I wish to make deals with Mr de Waal's statement that 'It is quite possible that Operation Restore Hope did save hundreds of thousands of lives. But no one can be sure.' I believe Mr de Waal is correct. The intervention did save hundreds of thousands of lives, but it cannot be proven because we do not have a measurement that is foolproof in predicting that this child or that adult would have died had they not been helped.

In his concluding paragraph, Mr de Waal asks: 'Can the NGOs really call for the military occupation of a country with complete impunity?' In the entirety of CARE's history, and, to my knowledge, the history of other NGOs, we have never called for the military occupation of a country. Neither UNOSOM nor any NGO registered with UNOSOM has ever called for the US military or the Allies to militarily occupy Somalia. That is a total misreading of the motivation of the NGOs and the history of the events that took place in Somalia. ❏

In the entirety of CARE's history and the history of other NGOs, we have never called for the military occupation of a country

A dilemma

Ed Cairns, policy adviser, Oxfam, UK

Crises of violence and extreme suffering are now afflicting millions of people across the world. They find expression in complex emergencies which are the result of violent conflict, not natural disasters.

We are all still struggling to understand the precise causes, yet for organisations that seek to relieve suffering, the consequence is clear: a daunting range of practical and ethical challenges.

There is currently a profound debate concerning the provision of relief to some 630,000 Rwandese refugees in camps in eastern Zaire, now largely controlled by those who masterminded the genocidal slaughter of up to one million Rwandese between April and July 1994.

How can it be right for humanitarian agencies to provide aid to such people, particularly if the aid helps them to prepare for an armed return to Rwanda? Although abuse of aid is not new, and stems from the prevailing nature of conflict in which civilians are the prime target, surely Goma amounts to one of the gravest abuses of aid in modern times?

To answer this, we have to ask what agencies like Oxfam should be doing. Article Three of the Universal Declaration of Human Rights states: 'Everyone has the right to life, liberty and security of person.' While humanitarian agencies have traditionally seen these rights threatened by lack of material resources, human rights groups have focused on threats from the political actions of governments and others. Such compartments are no longer valid. Oxfam believes in the indivisibility of all rights: the right to relief, for example, is neither greater nor less than the right to protection from physical attack.

In Zaire and Tanzania a great number of humanitarian agencies have not just provided relief to the refugees, but also put great energy into calling for action to stop the genocide — and now to seek justice and an end to the control of the refugees by the killers.

Equally, however, emergencies in which starvation is the aim of a military strategy make a nonsense of looking at human rights as merely those traditionally labelled 'civil and political'. When suffering is at its most acute, the right to life also demands that rights to food and water are met. Rights must be a united, as well as universal, body of principle.

Goma illustrates why this is so difficult for humanitarian agencies to put into practice. The right to life is threatened both by a lack of relief and by the prospect of further conflict. Yet there is the clear tension between protecting people from the former threat without exacerbating the latter.

This dilemma is made more acute by the relative inaction of other parts of the 'international community'. It is the duty of governments hosting refugees, and the United Nations High Commissioner for Refugees, to determine which Rwandese now living in neighbouring countries are true 'refugees'. Dr Boutros-Ghali proposed to the Security Council that a security operation should be authorised to do this. Yet the governments who could deliver the resources see central Africa as peripheral to their interests.

As in Yugoslavia, aid agencies are in an invidious position when other, much more powerful actors fail to meet their obligations under international law.

As more and more aid is channelled through non-governmental organisations, we are in real danger of becoming the humanitarian cover for complete failure to address the more fundamental causes of conflicts.

How should we respond? Some people suggest that aid agencies should deny aid to people in the Goma camps suspected of human rights abuses. Yet aid agencies that adopt this approach are in danger of becoming judge, jury and executioner, meting out possible death sentences against individuals who have not had a fair trial, and inevitably withdrawing aid from the innocent.

In each case, we have to make painful judgements on what action will do most to relieve suffering, both in the short- and longer-terms. Our decisions must be guided by an honest pragmatism and humility (because all options have risks), and not by an ideological belief in the superiority of one body of rights over another.

'Humanitarian neutrality' is one such 'superiority' which may still be relevant for some organisations with specific mandates, but which the humanitarian community as a whole should now discard.

The challenge for humanitarian agencies is to guard against both complacency in traditional roles and despair at new roles demanded by 'complex emergencies'. Advocacy has to look further than direct obstacles to relief or development work to address the causes of suffering to ensure, for example, that those chiefly responsible for genocide are speedily prosecuted.

Increasingly, humanitarian agencies recognise that they are only one of many key actors, and that it is how these actors work together to promote people's rights that determines whether suffering is tackled effectively. ❏

Addendum
The full acknowledgements to 'Making waves' (*Index* 1/1995), the shortened version of the joint Article 19/*Index* report *Who Rules the Airwaves? Broadcasting in Africa*, should have included Article 19's grateful acknowledgement for the support of the Norwegian Ministry of Foreign Affairs; and *Index*'s thanks for the support of Danida, Norad and the European Commission for the research undertaken by Adewale Maja-Pearce and for the distribution of the publication in Africa. ❏

NEWS & MEDIA REVIEW

On the streets of Lima: fully armed and ready to go

CECILIA VALENZUELA

Find me a war

With elections due in April, the war with Ecuador has become President Fujimori's most powerful campaign tool

A well-known comic strip in a Lima daily recently showed President Fujimori asking a journalist on his re-election campaign trail: 'Do you promise to tell the truth, the whole truth, and nothing but the truth?' 'Yes, your honour,' the cartoon journalist replies. 'Then you're not coming along with me!' retorts the president.

The cartoon neatly encapsulates the way the government is now manipulating public opinion through television news and current affairs programmes.

For the last three years, Peru has been living under a subtle and well-managed dictatorship. The president of the republic, constitutionally elected in 1990, violated that same Constitution in 1992 when, with the help of the military, he instigated a *coup d'état*, closed down Congress and took over the judiciary. The only people with advance warning of Fujimori's surprise, were the proprietors of the country's television stations.

The National Intelligence Service gave Fujimori good advice on the management of a society predominantly concerned with survival: bribe media bosses, or pressurise them through official control over advertising. The mass media have been obedient spokesmen ever since, orchestrating the disinformation campaign that Fujimori needs to maintain his regime. Fujimori's government also retains the services of two public relations companies. Both have profited from lucrative contracts to represent Peru's biggest companies, public as well as private. As a result, their ability to influence the media agenda is enormous.

Most Latin American constitutions — with the exceptions of Argentina and now Peru — prohibit their presidents from serving two successive terms. In Peru the power of the executive is out of all proportion to that of the other branches of government, making it impossible to minimise the built-in advantages of an incumbent presidential candidate.

The National Electoral Commission — a fully autonomous body, according to the new Constitution — was set up to regulate the presidential re-election campaign, thereby guaranteeing conditions of equality for the other candidates. The pro-Fujimori majority in Congress, however, set the commission on the right track by refusing to pass the electoral law unamended. As it stood, they argued, the law would have 'imprisoned' Fujimori in the presidential palace.

So the president was allowed to continue on the campaign trail, touring the country in the presidential plane or in army helicopters, handing out election leaflets at rallies orchestrated by military personnel. And always accompanied by a select group of reporters accredited by the palace.

He was also allowed to interfere unchecked in the campaigns of his opponents. Javier Perez de Cuellar was surprised early on in the campaign, at a rally in Cuzco's main square, to see a group of supposed supporters bearing placards that read: 'Perez de Cuellar, the Shining Path Communist Party salutes and supports you.'

But on 26 January the course of the campaign suddenly altered: overnight Peru had become embroiled in cross-border war with neighbouring Ecuador. This was no simple border skirmish. While neither party admits to firing the first shot across the disputed territory, they have, between them, brought their countries to the brink of total war.

After almost three weeks of fierce fighting, Fujimori announced that the invading Ecuadorian army had been successfully repelled and declared a unilateral ceasefire. He also signed a peace accord that, according to most analysts, was far from being in the country's best interests.

Nothing could have been further from the truth: Fujimori's announcement of victory was calculated to increase his standing in the opinion polls and it soon became clear from sources in the army that Ecuador's most important strategic positions had not been, and would not be, retaken. The fighting continued and the numbers of dead and wounded mounted up.

At which point, Javier Perez de Cuellar announced that, given the situation, he would not continue with his campaign. The other candidates also became markedly more muted and all the opposition groups agreed that it would be more seemly to put the interests of the nation above partisan politics.

Fujimori saw no conflict of interest between his election campaign and his conduct of the war. Nor did he see any need to keep Congress or the other presidential candidates informed about the progress of events. By default, Fujimori became the only presidential candidate still widely visible in the media — in his role as president.

With a permanent smile glued to his face, Fujimori tours the villages of Peru's northeastern border zone, accompanied by his favourite and most loyal reporters. Independent reporters are routinely denied a place on the presidential bandwagon and on official press tours of the area around the Rio Cenepa, where the war is most fierce.

The loyal press have presented these tours of the war zone as martial epics with a heroic protagonist, disguising the reality of a war that is maiming the countryside. The electoral value of such excursions, however, has not gone unremarked in certain sectors of the independent press.

The conflict with Ecuador exposes Fujimori's lack of scruple. It also highlights the submission of those substantial sectors of the media, whose lack of scruple matches that of the president, and who promote his electoral interests regardless of the facts. ❑

Translated by Adam Newey

VERA RICH

Never mind the language

On 14 May the people of Belarus will participate in their first fully democratic parliamentary election. But without an independent press, the odds on a fair contest are not good

Belarus's outgoing parliament, elected in March 1990, is the last of the old Supreme Soviets. Like all those assemblies, it includes a number of 'reserved' seats for special-interest groups and the 1990 rules for the election campaign gave a built-in advantage to the Communists. Out of a total of 360 seats, fewer than 40 'democrats' were elected.

The May elections will no doubt fulfil the criteria of the international observers. But, say Belarusian democrats, the campaign will lack one of the essential ingredients of true democracy: an independent mass-circulation press and equal access for all parties to TV and radio.

In Belarus, all mass-circulation papers are to a considerable extent controlled by the government: it subsidises them financially and, though soaring inflation has rendered this nugatory, expects that editorial policy will toe the government line.

Independent newspapers are legal in Belarus, but shortage of cash and paper supplies limits them to occasional and weekly publications. Moreover, there is only one printing house in Belarus with anything approaching modern technology, the Dom Druku. In the run-up to the presidential elections of 1994, the independent Belarusian-language weekly, *Svaboda* (Freedom), was on several occasions warned by the Dom Druku that 'pressure of work' made it impossible to guarantee future production. The only alternatives are either to print abroad, which means paying in hard currency, or to find some friendly, but technologically obsolescent, provincial printer.

The election of the populist Alaksandr Lukasenka as president in July 1994 did not improve the situation. Lukasenka ran on a platform of economic reform and the fight against corruption, but has made little progress on either front. A team of some 200 legal experts sympathetic to the Popular Front recently began an investigation into allegations of corruption against the president's own, supposedly whiter-than-white, team.

On 21 December 1994, Siarhiej Antoncyk, a democratic MP, began to read the lawyers' report to the House. The government's reaction was swift: broadcasting equipment in the chamber was switched off and, the following day, leading newspapers appeared with blank spaces.

Over the next few days some leading dailies failed to appear at all. The impending Christmas holidays, and the focus of world attention on Chechnya, made it impossible for Belarusian human rights activists to mobilise support abroad.

President Lukasenka, meanwhile, in an end-of-year address to the nation, denied that there had been any media clampdown — though copies of the censored editions were still available on some newsstands. At the same time, the president ordered the dismissal of the editor-in-chief of *Sovietskaya Belarussia,* the leading Russian-language daily, ostensibly for irregular hard-currency dealings, in reality on account of the Antoncyk affair, and the paper's stated intention of renouncing the government subsidy.

The Antoncyk report was eventually printed in full by *Svaboda* in a special edition printed, apparently, abroad. As a result, *Svaboda* lost its contract with the Dom Druku, as did three other independent Russian-language papers, *Femida, Belorusskaya Delovaya Gazeta* and *Gazeta Andreya Klimova.*

The attack on the Russian-language press, provoked by the Antoncyk affair made it clear that the president and his team are unwilling to tolerate any media criticism, no matter the language in which it is couched. Lukasenka and his team, no less than the ex-Communists in parliament, advocate close ties with Russia, and want to give the Russian language official status alongside Belarusian. ❏

JAMES D ROSS

Pressed into action

The continuing battle over Cambodia's new press law is testing the mettle of a fragile democracy

Democratic government did not come to Cambodia following the UN-supervised elections in May 1993. A power-sharing arrangement, brokered by King Sihanouk between the election-winning Funcinpec party of his son Norodom Ranariddh and the former ruling Communist Cambodian People's Party (CPP) led by Hun Sen, legitimised the pre-election status quo. The result is a government that differs in appearance, but little in substance, from the authoritarian regime that existed before the UN arrived.

Even the most optimistic did not expect Cambodia to become a fully functioning democracy overnight, but popular hopes that Funcinpec would seriously address the country's corruption and development problems have been dashed. Much of the blame lies with Prime Minister Norodom Ranariddh, who has placed personal financial gain before the development of a strong and democratically viable Funcinpec party. Funcinpec's National Assembly members have been warned repeatedly to toe the coalition government's line or face expulsion from the Assembly.

But the UN's presence did help create a more open political climate in Phnom Penh. Since 1992, more than two dozen Khmer-language newspapers have started up. Local human rights groups report on rampant violations by the police and military, as well as on Khmer Rouge atrocities. And dozens of new non-governmental organisations are starting to displace their international counterparts in development and educational projects and are speaking out on issues of concern.

Over the past year, the main battles for control over 'democratic space' in Cambodia have been fought over press freedom. Stories appear daily, castigating corruption and incompetence by government officials, from ministers, governors and generals downwards. Their crusading style has been marred by poor journalism skills: rumour is published as fact and little effort is made to substantiate sources. But the press has provided a much-needed check on the government.

The government, in turn, has suspended nine newspapers during the last 12 months, typically for articles and cartoons suggesting corruption in high places. Nguon Nonn, the controversial editor of the *Morning News*, was jailed following his paper's publication of articles implicating high-level CPP officials in the failed coup attempt of July 1994.

Two politically motivated murders have added considerably to the nervousness of the local press corps. Nonn Chan, editor of the outspoken *Voice of Khmer Youth*, was gunned down in Phnom Penh on 7 September; and journalist Sao Chan Dara, who had been investigating illegal logging in Kompong Cham province, was shot dead in December, allegedly by a military officer who had been implicated in the articles. Both men had reported receiving death threats from government officials.

The government further expressed its displeasure with the press in its amendments to the new press law drafted early in 1994 by the National Assembly's Human Rights Committee. This was intended to codify the protections for freedom of expression in the new Constitution, but by the time the Information Ministry had finished with it, the law included broadly worded restrictions on the media that echoed past Communist practices. Protests from the Khmer Journalists' Association and human rights groups in Cambodia and abroad eventually compelled the government to reconsider its draft.

A new version, strongly opposed by local journalists and human rights groups, was passed by the Council of Ministers in November. Despite some improvements, it carried tough criminal penalties, including prison sentences of up to five years, for a

wide range of vaguely worded offences, such as publishing articles that 'humiliate national organs or public authorities'.

At the end of December, after months of lobbying, King Sihanouk issued a statement opposing criminal penalties for journalists. Soon after, Prime Minister Ranariddh reiterated his father's view, a surprising about-face from one of the chief proponents of a strict press law. When National Assembly chairman Chea Sim, CPP leader and widely regarded

Phnom Penh 1993: Funcinpec fails to deliver

as the most powerful man in the country, also expressed support for the King's position, it seemed that no-one had ever really wanted criminal penalties in the first place.

The draft press law is expected to be a priority when the National Assembly reconvenes in late March. The criminal penalties and much of the vague language in the bill will probably be eliminated.

Meanwhile, in February the government suspended one newspaper, confiscated another and sentenced a journalist to one year in jail for disinformation. But the battle over the press law suggests that despite a worsening political environment, concerted grassroots activism can get results. The future of Cambodia's democracy will depend on it. ❑

CECILE MARCEL

A home-grown affair

Despite official claims to the contrary, the three-month-old protest movement in Bahrain continues

After a quiet February, the authorities in Bahrain were once again shaken by renewed violence in the dominantly Shi'ite areas of this tiny Gulf state. According to eyewitnesses, on 2 March, police opened fire on a crowd of around 3,000 in the Sitra region again protesting the government's violent repression of the broad-based pro-democracy move-

ment, 'killing two and injuring scores more'. The demonstration was the largest since 27 January when protests apparently petered out in the wake of the deportation of the movement's leaders earlier in the month. From its exile base in London, the Islamic Front for the Liberation of Bahrain, confirmed the above and added that there had been other simultaneous demonstrations 'in other Shi'ite villages'.

Trouble first erupted on 5 December 1994 when Sheikh Ali Salman, a 29-year-old cleric and one of the leaders of the pro-democracy movement calling for the restoration of parliament, was arrested in a dawn raid on his house. His arrest sparked a wave of protests throughout the country in which at least seven people were killed by the security forces, scores of others injured and more than 2,300 arrested. Those who have been released report torture, refusal of medical care and the sexual abuse of children while in custody.

Demonstrations and disturbances, which continued sporadically for almost two months and were violently quelled by the security forces, had originated in a petition, signed by more than 25,000 people, calling for the restoration of the constitutional institutions in abeyance since 1974. As the protest spread, the movement also demanded the release of political prisoners, an end to forced deportations and the repeal of the State Security Law.

Deportation has been the means by which the rulers of Bahrain dispose of troublemakers. Throughout

January, leaders of the pro-democracy movement were deported from Bahrain, among them, on 15 January, Sheikh Ali Salman. Forcible exile of its nationals is in breach of Bahrain's Constitution as well as the Universal Declaration of Human Rights.

As the disturbances continued, the government attempted to reassure its regional partners and, more important, foreign investors by means of a widespread disinformation campaign. It has been well known since independence in 1971 that Bahrain would be the first — maybe the only — Gulf oil producer to face a future without oil. As a result, it has depended heavily on regional stability and international confidence to build up and finance an alternative economic structure. The government-dominated media claimed the disturbances were instigated by Iranian-backed fundamentalists, denounced foreign media coverage of the continuing confrontation, and promoted a picture of a contented population — 60 per cent of which is Shia — united behind its government's denunciation of 'alien elements from abroad'.

In fact, there is no lack of discontent at home. In 1974, to silence growing parliamentary protests against a law granting the government broad powers over state security, Emir al Sheikh Isa Bin Salman al-Khalifa dissolved the National Assembly and suspended several articles of the Constitution. Since then, the Emir has ruled by decree, with members of his family occupying key ministerial positions. After a first petition protesting this in 1992, he created a 'Consultative Council'. This has done nothing to reduce human rights abuses: the State Security Law, for instance, permits arbitrary arrest, detention and torture, and allows for the detention of suspects for up to three years without charge or trial. All political rights are suspended.

The economic situation has also deteriorated dramatically and the impact of rising unemployment is felt most severely by the Shia population; over the years, the government has failed to address problems created by discrimination, corruption and a labour market that depends heavily on expatriate workers. ❑

GITOBU IMANYARA

Judicial charades

Koigi wa Wamwere is on trial for his life in Kenya. Both trial and charges are rigged

In November last year, Amnesty International persuaded the British prime minister, John Major, to raise the case of Koigi wa Wamwere with Kenyan President Daniel arap Moi during one of his increasingly rare trips to western capitals. Despite a long history of miscarriages of justice, unlawful arrest and years in prison without trial, Moi is reported to have promised that Koigi wa Wamwere would, finally, get a 'fair trial'. A verdict is expected some time in May but if Koigi wa Wamwere is freed, it is likely to be because Moi is more

HOWARD DAVIES/AMNESTY INTERNATIONAL

Koigi wa Wamwere

susceptible to pressure from the IMF and the donor community than to respect for the law in his own country.

Koigi wa Wamwere is a long-term opponent of the policies of the Kenya African National Union (KANU), the ruling party since independence from Britain in 1963. He has spent close to 10 years in prison without ever being convicted of any crime, and has never advocated the violent overthrow of the government. His trial is an example of the manner in which the Kenyan government cynically manipulates the legal process for political ends.

Shortly after his election to the Nakuru North constituency in 1975, Koigi was locking horns with the government over his pet subject — land policy and the resettlement of the landless in the Rift Valley province. In August 1975 the government of President Jomo Kenyatta

detained Koigi to prevent him raising embarrassing land issues in parliament. He remained in prison until Kenyatta's death in August 1978.

Following a failed coup attempt by junior officers of the Kenya Air Force in 1982, the new government of President Moi launched a major crackdown on its opponents. Koigi was again among those arrested and detained without trial until December 1984. He again lost his seat.

When the seat fell vacant Koigi, a Kikuyu, was warned not to seek elective office in the Rift Valley, which was now reserved for President Moi's Kalenjin tribesmen. By this time Moi had begun to implement his *majimbo* policies — a form of ethnic purification designed to rid the Rift Valley province of its non-Kalenjin inhabitants. Moi's closest confidante and Kenya's most feared politician, Nicholas Biwott — later to be named prime suspect in the grisly murder of Foreign Affairs Minister Robert Ouko — went as far as promising Koigi 'any amount of money or any other public office' if he would agree to quit Rift Valley politics. Koigi refused but lost in a contest that was clearly rigged.

With the collapse of Communism and the imminent release of the world's most prominent political prisoner, Nelson Mandela, the traditional Kenyan allies in western capitals began to take a keener interest in the goings-on in Kenya. Responding to pressure from the World Bank, the IMF and the Kenyan donor community, Moi reluctantly allowed the registration of opposition parties.

Travelling from Norway where he had taken refuge in 1986, Koigi arrived in the Kenya/Uganda border town of Busia in August 1990. A month later he was kidnapped and found himself back in the torture chambers of the notorious Nyayo House where he was 'welcomed back, severely tortured and asked to admit that what Kenyans need most is terror and not democracy...'

The interrogation and torture lasted a month before he, together with two lawyers and a number of relatives, was charged with treason. Kenya's state-owned propaganda machine went into full gear: President Moi announced that Koigi had been arrested 'with 10 guns and 10 grenades of a new variety intended to maim and kill people and children'. The charges facing Koigi and his co-accused stated they were 'planning and organising throughout Kenya to rob individuals, shops, public transport and banks to finance the overthrow of the government'.

The trial dragged on until January 1993, when President Moi ordered Attorney General Amos Wako to drop the charges. Koigi and his colleagues were freed after more than two years in prison. Koigi left Kenya for Norway, returning in May 1993 to announce the formation of the National Democratic Human Rights Organisation (NDEHURIO) to campaign for greater respect for human rights in Kenya. On 18 September 1993, he was again arrested and accused of illegal entry into special security zones of the Rift Valley province. He was denied bail.

On 19 October 1993 the magistrate ordered that Koigi and his co-accused deposit their passports with the court and report twice a week to the police in Nakuru. The police immediately sought a review of this order and the magistrate announced a he ruling for 1 November.

On 1 November, Koigi travelled to Nakuru from Nairobi to hear the magistrate refuse his application for the return of his passport. He left court and went back to Nairobi, where he spent the night in the house of his lawyer, Gibson Kamau Kuria. Kuria has sworn an affidavit that Koigi could not, therefore, have been in Nakuru on the night of 1 and 2 November when it is alleged that he and his relatives Geoffrey Njugura Ngengi, Charles Kuria Wamwere and James Maigua committed armed robbery at Bahati police station. They have now spent more than a year in custody on this charge and of possessing firearms without a certificate.

The charges carry a mandatory death sentence. Despite overwhelming evidence of their innocence, Koigi wa Wamwere and his colleagues continue to face a carefully orchestrated judicial charade. Independent legal observers worldwide have dismissed the trial as a farce. In the latest of such reports, Article 19 states that the 'extraordinarily misdirected proceedings which only serve to undermine the dignity of the judicial process in Kenya, appear to lead inexorably towards their conviction and imposition of the death sentence.' ❑

Liberty in Britain

In a report jointly compiled and edited with Matthew Hoffman of the *Independent, Index* examines a society caught between a culture of secrecy and the citizen's right to know

NICK COBBING

DIEU ET MON RIGHT-TO-KNOW

MATTHEW HOFFMAN

Freedom's inhibitions

In 1988, Ronald Dworkin wrote in these pages that under the then Thatcher government 'a worrying attack' was taking place 'on the whole culture of liberty, on the special and honoured place of freedom in democracy'. Although I edited the edition of *Index* about censorship in Britain (*Index* 8/1988) in which these words appeared, and shared to a degree the worries of our contributors about a many-sided assault on free expression, I allowed myself the hope in my introduction that what we were actually seeing were faltering attempts by government to contain a wider demand for information from the citizenry and the media.

Seven years on, there is still no Freedom of Information Act, although there is now an ineffectual post of minister for 'open government'; libel laws have not been reformed; and there is a new threat from politicians to legislate a 'right of privacy' against press attention to the personal lives of private and public figures, such as themselves. The last of these demands follows in good part from the exposure by the press, after John Major's call for a return to 'basics' in the country's standards, of the less-than-edifying sexual and financial activities of some of his own junior ministers.

I now suspect, as Mark Fisher argues in these pages, that the British at large, despite showing a great appetite for reading about the private shenanigans of their Royal Family, pop and TV stars, and even their neighbours, do not particularly value the right to satisfy these appetites. They feel somewhat ashamed of their 'prurient' interests, and so they tell pollsters that they wish to see such publications restricted — but continue to provide their market. To date, the Major government, while not moving in a liberalising direction, has resisted the call for new restrictive laws on the press, partially because such reforms as a law of privacy would look like an attempt to protect its own members' behaviour from press scrutiny.

In addition, with a small and divided majority, the government fears to take a controversial stance on any matter. Nonetheless, one feels that were there to be a public furore over some sensational revelation that brought out strong, if passing, support for a tough privacy law (for example, something shameful written about the Queen herself), MPs on both sides of the house would be only too happy to oblige. And, of course, there would be no entrenched constitutional provision for the protection of free speech to restrain them.

Without constitutional restraints on MPs, only what Ronald Dworkin refers to as a 'quasi-religious standing' for liberty among the populace at large could be counted on to protect a free, inquiring press from such new fetters. But there is little evidence of a pervasive political and social culture in Britain that values freedom of expression as a first-order value, above the hurt and discomfort that its uninhibited exercise is bound to entail. The following pages show that whether it be broadcast television, videos, public demonstrations or investigative journalism, the urge to censor is at least as great as it was seven years ago. Indeed, a dismal consensus on the need to impose further social controls seems to unite politicians and commentators from left, right and centre. ❑

MARK FISHER

Virtual liberty

Is liberty alive in Britain? Are our freedoms and rights real and effective? Or do we live in a state of virtual liberty, all appearance but little substance?

Political changes in various parts of the world — Mrs Thatcher's and John Major's cutting back of the state in Britain; the rise of Newt Gingrich and the New Right in the USA; the collapse of the Left in Italy; the emergence of new democracies in eastern Europe — are forcing questions about the nature of liberty to the centre of public debate. In all these countries liberty has become a political battleground, with both Left and Right claiming to be its guardian.

The classic liberal position — that both individual and collective freedoms are best secured by rights enshrined in laws, all of which have necessary limitations and restraints to ensure a balance between protective freedom and abusive licence — is being dismantled. This raises fundamental questions. What is the relationship between political and economic freedom? Or between individual and collective rights? In what respect is the state the guarantor of freedoms, or the creator of restraints? To what extent is liberty expressed in a state of mind, or in a body of laws? By what criteria should we adjudicate when different freedoms conflict? For whom should freedom exist? To think, to say and to do what? And who decides?

The Right insists that social legislation, including the protection of collective and individual rights, has created neither equity nor efficiency. It claims that an individual can better exercise freedom of choice by being economically liberated through the market. This fusion of social and economic freedoms relies on a sleight of hand that uses Britain's lack of national economic success as an excuse to attack fundamental social rights, while claiming a new age of freedom from bureaucratic regulation and a rolling back of the state. Not surprisingly, the beneficiaries of this

London 1994: democracy is the right to demonstrate...

have been companies, not individuals.

What is notable about this tradition is its inconsistency. Economic *laissez-faire* liberalism has not been matched by social libertarianism. On the contrary, economic deregulation has been accompanied by social authoritarianism. Unlike its counterpart in the USA, the British government continues to control information and maintains some of the strictest libel laws in any western democracy. It has introduced legislation restricting the 'promotion' of gay or lesbian lifestyles, established the Broadcasting Standards Council to preview and 'maintain' standards in television, and imposed a whole new range of constraints on people's lives in the new Criminal Justice Act, particularly those of squatters, travellers and demonstrators.

When the CJA came into effect in February, important and ancient rights were amended or removed, most damagingly the right to assemble and the right to silence. The freedom to combine, to take secondary supportive action and to peacefully protest in industrial disputes had already been severely curtailed by the government's reforms to trade union law. The 1986 Public Order Act restricted behaviour on all types of demonstrations by making the use of 'abusive' or 'insulting' language or actions an offence whether anyone was, in practice, abused or insulted.

Our immigration laws are being implemented in increasingly harsh ways: innocent people are deported, the freedom of people to come to Britain to live with their spouse, even when that person is a British citizen, is being restricted by the 'primary purpose' rule.

Most shameful of all is the government's treatment of those people, subject to imprisonment or torture for their beliefs or their views in their own country, who turn to Britain for political asylum. The existence of detention centres like Campsfield and Rickmansworth, imprisoning hundreds of political refugees, is sharply at odds with the image of Britain, still common both here and abroad, as an open liberal democracy.

More objective and damning evidence can be found in Britain's recent record as an infringer of human rights in the European Court in Strasbourg where no other country has as bad a record or has committed as many serious breaches of the European Convention on Human Rights as the UK: racial discrimination, interrogation methods and the Diplock courts in Northern Ireland, sex discrimination in immigration control, unlawful phone tapping, interference with prisoners' letters, the rights of

...and the right to shelter

mental patients. It is no coincidence that, alone among the 26 member states, Britain does not have an enforceable Bill of Rights.

In a democracy there are two forms of protection against governments that are indifferent to human rights: officials prepared to blow the whistle, and media willing to publicise government excesses. After civil servants Clive Ponting and Sarah Tisdall had publicly criticised their ministerial masters in 1984, the government introduced an Official Secrets Act that denied civil servants the right to make public any abuses or mismanagement in their departments even if such disclosure was in the public interest, and reinforced this elsewhere in the public sector by means of codes of professional conduct with 'gagging clauses' that made confidentiality a condition of employment.

The media have been less directly, but no less effectively, inhibited by an aggressive use of contempt of court laws under which journalists, and in 1993 the television company Channel 4, were taken to court for refusing to reveal their sources, and by the use of libel laws that frequently protect the actions of the rich and powerful from public scrutiny. At the same time, the unleashing of market forces in both the press and broadcasting has encouraged some editors and producers to give priority to profits rather than to investigative journalism.

But it is too simplistic to attribute all the blame for the erosion of our liberties to an arrogant government or to constrained media. Too often we have, as a nation, sat in silence and watched as our liberties disappeared. There has been little sense of public outrage and only occasional and spasmodic protest. We have been poor guardians of our own freedoms. What happened to the tradition of dissent in Britain?

But this begs a further question: would we regain a positive sense of liberty if a future government stitched together the web of rights that has been undone over the past 15 years?

If liberty is fully expressed by legal guarantees and rights, then the answer must be 'yes'. But in practice, many of our freedoms depend on an individual having the power or money to exercise them. What value the legal right to clear your good name against misrepresentation or libel if you cannot cover the legal costs? What virtue in the government's freedoms of choice in health or education if the fees are beyond your means?

There is another problem. Rights on the statute book and the effective means of realising them, are simply the mechanics of liberty. For a society truly to be free, it must feel itself free, it must be free in its mind. And we are not.

We suffer from several peculiarly British vices: a sense of historic arrogance that breeds complacency and, above all, an over-developed and suffocating sense of deference — to those in authority, to those with money, to those with professional qualifications. It has given us stability but no sense of equality, let alone the bloody-mindedness that asserts and extends its rights.

The reasons for this are buried in our history: in the continuity of land owning; in the hereditary system; in the evolutionary nature of common law; in having a ruling class that has proved sufficiently adaptable to ensure its survival; in some innate conservatism that has absorbed the sparks of political or industrial fervour — the Chartists, trades unions, the suffragettes — rather than let them catch fire; in our avoidance of a revolution. We have favoured the comforts of fairness rather than the uncertainties of freedom.

This lack of collective 'attitude' inhibits us from asking some basic questions. Why are so few women in positions of power or authority? Why is there so little industrial democracy? Why do we tolerate such low levels of active participation in public life? Why are we denied basic rights such as access to all our personal records held by the state? Why, in short, do we continue to be the objects of government rather than its masters? We put these hawsers on our minds, ensuring that the rights we do have are not enjoyed in practice, trapping us in virtual liberty.

We must create a new framework of rights, adding some (such as the right to freedom of information), strengthening others (such as the right to equality of opportunity and non-discrimination), restoring those that have been amended or undermined (such as the right to silence) and setting them all within a new Bill of Rights that incorporates international agreements on human rights. And we must strengthen the economy so that access to those rights that depend on money for their effectiveness is widened.

But liberty, in the end, is a state of mind, not a gift of government. We have to begin to want and to value it; to demand and, when necessary, to dissent; to be bold in claiming it. Only then shall we begin to turn the shadows of virtual liberty into the substance of the thing itself. ❏

ALAN CLARK

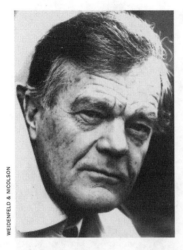

The uses and abuses of secrecy

'Censorship' is one of those terms like 'fascist' or 'politically correct' that have slid downwards into the pool of all-purpose pejoratives, whose deployment can often indicate little more than generalised distaste of hostility.

I regard it as meaning the denial, or interdiction of information by decree (usually Order in Council, occasionally by Statute) when applied by government. The term *can* be stretched to include deliberate omission or distortion of 'news' by private or corporate pressure, or the threat of civil damages, but I would like first to look at censorship by government.

In my view this is justifiable in two categories only, and they should be drawn as narrowly as possible.

First the vexatious heading of 'National Security'.

Most people would accept that technical Service information — the operational charts of ocean-going submarines; codes and cyphers; key sequences in electronic counter-measure, for example — are properly kept secret. And in the Intelligence field there is a duty lying on the authorities to protect as best they can the lives (and thus usually the identities) of their agents.

The second function of government where a measure of censorship is

House of Commons terrace: behind the corridors of power

legitimate (but where, I am sorry to say, it is often abused) is that classified as 'commercial confidentiality'. Plainly where an investor with prior knowledge could make a fast profit — ministerial procurement contracts, referrals to the Monopolies and Mergers Commission are two obvious headings — the authorities have an equitable duty to avoid premature disclosure.

There are three other categories where governments do practice, or at least attempt to apply, censorship. In my view quite wrongly and often under the pretence that one or both of the two 'primary' considerations apply. These are — administrative convenience; public reputation (of ministers or officials); and personal embarrassment.

Most MP's are slack and incompetent, if not actually venal, in their operation of the procedure for parliamentary questions. They draft usually on the basis of getting a headline that will, if noticed by their constituents, indicate 'activity'. Some table, or get their researchers to draft, hundreds. Some occasionally perk up a bit and take (extra) money for so doing.

But practically none — Tam Dalyell is the most effective and persistent but Nicholas Budgen and Richard Shepherd are also 'dangerous' — has mastered the technique of repeated interrogation. How to use last week's ministerial answer as the building block for next week's question.

But if you have worked in a minister's outer office you will know the flap that precedes 'First for Questions'.

An apprehension not just that the minister will fluff his answer. But that something might be 'given away' that will lead to more work; establishment (or erosion) of 'precedent'; even a reproachful note from the permanent — or, still worse, the cabinet — secretary.

And all because of this one critical pitfall — a minister must not lie to the House of Commons.

If he does, he's out. The same day.

As a result every Question Time is a potential bout of arm-wrestling between the established order and those who have the capability, though very seldom it seems the inclination, to discover the truth. I always found it strange that MPs did so little to press their advantage here. I never saw officials actually repress information, although sometimes they would withhold it — *passim* Sir Robin Butler 'Truth can be no more than half the picture.' But here no reform is needed except to the intelligence and tenacity of those who are entitled to put the questions.

The fourth category which, as a historian I have always found particularly irritating (and which of course often overlaps with that of administrative convenience) is the protection of reputations. And, as we know, it can be extended from the reputation of a deceased functionary into a general susceptibility to the feelings of relatives, and even surviving offspring.

The arguments are well-rehearsed. They are deployed to justify the 30 year rule (too often extended to 50 years, sometimes to total excision and destruction of documents). Freedom of discussion and the quality of official advice would be inhibited if the participants thought that their fallibility might, with hindsight, be prematurely (sic) revealed.

This is completely bogus.

The fact that the public are not allowed to know the truth about cabinet discussion of peace terms with Hitler; or the contents of Rudolf Hess's brief which he brought on his mission in 1941; or the wartime antics and financial speculations of the Duke of Windsor; or the full degree of pressure applied by the Americans to sterling over Suez; or the text of the consultations during the Cuban missile crisis, is nothing to do with *personal* reputations. Far more is it a kind of general 'not-in-the-public interest' factor.

Most MPs are slack and incompetent, if not actually venal, in their operation of the procedure for parliamentary questions

Why not? one may ask. To which the only possible answers are (a) 'because *not*'; and (b) 'because it might lower the esteem in which you held your elders and betters.'

Unbelievably (b) is also deployed as a serious argument to justify the suppression of reportage (disreputable reportage only, of course) concerning the 'private lives' of politicians, members of the Royal Family and — sometimes it does seem — even the more prominent alumni of cafe society.

These are people who spend a large part of their own time writing personal press releases, searching for photo-opportunities, paying agencies to contrive or fabricate favourable 'publicity'. On what possible basis can they claim that they should enjoy some kind of immunity from comment if the technique goes occasionally wrong?

The last category, where I believe the arguments are more finely balanced, but which I approach with some diffidence as I have strong feelings but no expertise, is pornography.

I dislike the material intensely. Some of the most disagreeable intellectual experiences that I have had to endure as a Member of Parliament where the display of videos — suspiciously 'lifelike' — seized by the police, (and which they were subsequently forced by the courts to release), or appalling violence and sexual abuse committed against children and women.

My own common sense tells me that these films are an encouragement to commit crimes of a particularly cruel and degrading kind, and that both their manufacture and their distribution should be visited by heavy penalties.

But at the same time I recognise that many of the general convictions that I hold in rejecting most other forms of censorship may make this standpoint difficult to sustain in logic. ❏

© *Alan Clark*

POSY SIMMONDS

ANDREW PUDDEPHATT

Subject to erosion

In his first major speech, Lord Chief Justice Taylor said that Parliament was no longer capable of protecting people's rights and called for the incorporation of the European Convention on Human Rights into UK law. This unprecedented call from Britain's leading judge contrasts sharply with the traditional view that the political constitution established by the 1688 settlement is the best guarantor of our liberties. As Bill Walker MP said when moving a bill to reinforce the union with Scotland: 'Our constitution, although unwritten, gives us flexibility not enjoyed by countries with written constitutions. Citizens' rights are protected by the fact that Parliament is not bound by decisions made by previous Parliaments. If we get something wrong, as we often do, we can rectify it the following year.' John Patten MP has also spoken of liberties guaranteed by our culture to the extent that we do not need to rely on enforceable rights.

How can we reconcile these contrasting claims? What is the evidence? We remain a society obsessed with secrecy, a country where we are not allowed to know the results of safety tests on cars, aeroplanes or ships — or the results of tests on new drugs or consumer goods. We live in a country where over 160 programmes dealing with Northern Ireland have been banned since 1969, including a song about the Birmingham Six and a pop video showing a street scene in Belfast with armoured cars passing children playing.

The 1989 Official Secrets Act contains no provision for freedom of information and makes it an absolute criminal offence to disclose certain categories of information, while at the same time prohibiting a public interest defence or a defence that the information was already in the public domain. Successive judgments by the courts have extended control over journalists' activities. Through the *Spycatcher* case, governments won the power generally to injunct publications, and journalists have faced fines or imprisonment for refusing to disclose sources. The growing concentration of ownership in television, radio and the press threatens to undermine freedom of information and expression. Today, just four companies control more than 85 per cent of all daily and Sunday newspaper circulation. Over 80 per cent of the local press in Britain is controlled by 15 corporate owners. Of the national press, only the *Guardian* and the *Independent* are owned by companies that do not have major interests outside the media.

No longer is our privacy inviolate. The police currently hold records on between one in six and one in 10 of the population, including information on many people who have no criminal record. The government permits the police to collect information on people on the basis of their political beliefs, religious affiliation, sexual identity and alleged HIV status, even though people are not suspected of committing a crime and even though much of that information is unsubstantiated or circumstantial. There has been a phenomenal growth in video surveillance, with over 220 local schemes now in operation. However, no research has been done demonstrating the effectiveness of video surveillance, nor are there any statutory controls. The government is proposing to introduce an identity card scheme and has advanced plans for a government data network linking existing government databases together. The introduction of a Personal Identification Number is all that is now required to give any state official access to the most comprehensive range of information about any citizen in this country.

In recent years, there has been widespread debate about the problems of the criminal justice system, a debate that came to a head with the release of the Birmingham Six in March 1991 and the establishment of a Royal Commission on Criminal Justice. Contrary to the views of this commission (and the previous Royal Commission on Criminal Procedure), the government has now restricted the exercise of the right to silence (*Index* 1&2/1994) to allow inferences to be drawn in the courts, with the possibility that should the

Heterosexual ... £25,000 p.a... asthmatic.. ..T.V licence dodger, 1992 .....Your tax disc is insecurely affixed to your windscreen, sir....

POSY SIMMONDS

accused choose not to speak, this could be used against him to infer guilt. This historic common law right, which can be traced back to John Lilburn and the treason trials of the Levellers in the seventeenth century, and which underpins the presumption of innocence, is now gone. The police have also been given a new stop and search power, including the authority to stop individuals without reasonable suspicion. The current climate of public concern about crime, a concern aided and abetted by private sector interests (who are marketing a range of security equipment and services), is leading to a growing demand for more punitive punishment of offenders despite all the evidence that such punishment is counter-productive. Certain categories of people can find themselves without adequate legal rights, particularly asylum seekers, refugees, and those suspected of being illegal immigrants. More and more discretionary power is being placed in the hands of the authorities, thus tilting the crucial balance between individual and state that lies at the heart of our criminal justice system.

The 1994 Criminal Justice and Public Order Act introduces new powers to restrict people's rights to protest. For the first time in British law, the police have been given the power to ban public meetings if they constitute 'trespassory assemblies'. This is despite assurances given by government ministers during the passage of the 1986 Public Order Act (when further restrictions on marches were introduced) that there was no intention of introducing controls on meetings because they were so fundamental to a democracy. A new criminal offence of aggravated trespass

London 1994: stop and search

has also been created. This allows the police to arrest demonstrators who are on land without permission, and who — in the view of the police — intend to disrupt the activities of others. Such powers, given that no land in this country is in common ownership, strike at the very heart of the legitimate right to protest. Although it might be argued the police have only used these powers against hunt saboteurs, it is uncomfortable to be living in a society where the exercise of such a fundamental right depends on the discretion of the police.

The same legislation also attacked the rights of other groups whose lifestyle was considered problematic for the authorities. The local authority obligation to provide travellers' sites was abolished and new punitive powers were introduced allowing travellers' homes to be seized if they camped on land without permission. For the first time in British law, an attempt has been made to define a kind of music — one that is characterised 'by the emission of a series of repetitive beats' — and subject it to legal controls. The police can enter the site where such music is playing, demand people leave, seize, impound and destroy equipment and establish cordons for up to five miles around the site of the alleged 'rave' to prevent people from travelling through. These are extraordinary powers to apply to a cultural development. We are a society prepared to tolerate the disruption caused by football matches, horse racing, motor racing and many other forms of social activity, but not that caused by one type of music.

In recent years, we have seen a debate spring up about 'political correctness' that has often become a coded attack on policies designed to tackle inequality and discrimination. Such a debate has concealed the fact that inequality and discrimination are now more rooted in our society than for many years. The level of racial violence against black people is growing: the Race Relations Act has not proved strong enough to check it. Women continue to experience widespread discrimination in public life and in employment. Despite laws prohibiting discrimination in employment and pay, there is a substantial gap in average gross hourly earnings between men and women. Britain has the highest earnings gap between men and women of all the major countries in the European Union.

Nor is discrimination confined to the black community and to

Continued on page 40

This is a Placard
NOT
A
PISTOL

...and Peaceful Protest is a threat to no one !

ELLIE CRONIN

Criminal?

I was on the Dole
3 hungry Children
2 bedroom Council flat
1 Income

Happy
Beautiful
Serene
Surroundings

I hated London
Selfish slum
Everybody out for themselves
No time to spare

Peace, tranquility
New life
Our own community
Living for the moment

Skyscrapers lurking
Over a polluted landscape
Factories pumping
Air Quality: Poor

We travelled together
Restoring Britain
Protecting habitats
Preserving life

Unemployment at its peak
I try
The recessions neverending
No money!

Loving, caring friends
Helping one another
We were happy
And Free!

Thats why we left

Our whole world Shattered.

The rainbow tribe
Our new home.

Moved on
Forced out
Packed up
Cleared off

Nowhere to go
Threatened at all times
Scared
Tired.

Made to leave our home
Intimidating landowners
Police
The earth belongs to all

Arrested
Homeless

Criminal?

Nowhere to rest
Life spent in our violet van
Turtle

by Ellie Cronin

NICK COBBING

Continued from page 37

women. Lesbians and gay men continue to experience employment discrimination and the age of consent for gay men has not been equalised with heterosexuals despite considerable pressure from campaign groups. An attempt to introduce a comprehensive anti-discrimination bill to prohibit discrimination on the grounds of disability was talked out in the House of Commons by government back-benchers, despite overwhelming popular support. For many people in our society, discrimination is not a political cause, it is a fact of life.

The conflict in Northern Ireland, prior to the current ceasefire, has given rise to a battery of emergency laws. Some, like the Emergency Provisions Act, are specific to Northern Ireland. This Act suspends the right to a jury trial for a whole schedule of offences, permits internment without trial and introduces special rules of evidence that would not be permitted in Britain. The Prevention of Terrorism Act applies to the UK as a whole. It allows detention without charge for up to seven days despite European Court rulings to the contrary. It allows for the prohibition of organisations and permits people to be excluded from Britain, Northern Ireland or the UK as a whole if they are not British residents, even though no charges are brought against the individual concerned and no evidence is produced to sustain those charges. Such powers have always been controversial and there is little evidence that their employment has seriously curtailed terrorist activity — indeed many would argue that they have fuelled resentment, particularly in the nationalist communities of Northern Ireland. The ceasefire is an opportunity to remove all emergency laws, and it is therefore disturbing to see new emergency powers incorporated in the recent Criminal Justice and Public Order Act, allowing police new powers of random stop and search for anti-terrorist purposes.

The picture above is inevitably cursory and could not claim to be a comprehensive survey of the state of our civil liberties. It does, however, underline recent calls for a Bill of Rights to be introduced into Britain — to put in place a legal framework which can be used to defend basic civil liberties from executive attack. In the past we may have relied upon our culture as the primary defence against loss of freedom, but it is clear that our culture, like the coastline, is subject to erosion. These days, our freedoms may require stronger support. ❏

HELENA KENNEDY

Who needs a Bill of Rights?

POSY SIMMONDS

The European Court of Human Rights is finally hearing a case that originated in events seven years ago when three IRA members were shot dead by the SAS in Gibraltar. Their relatives claim the British government was operating a shoot to kill policy and the shootings provoked consternation and debate, followed by outrage from the government over the Thames TV programme 'Death on the Rock'.

But for over seven years British people have not witnessed any objective examination of whether their government was operating a shoot to kill policy — a serious situation for people living in what we are repeatedly told is the cradle of democracy. Nothing connected with this case — apart from a Gibraltar inquest into the cause of death — has been addressed by a British court. The families of the dead have had no way of bringing an action against the British government on its own territory. None of us have this option — of challenging our government if we believe it has violated human rights. And it is this dangerous, undemocratic situation that must end.

It is ridiculous that in the period following World War II, Britain helped draft a Convention on Human Rights that it subsequently refused to incorporate into its own law. Such arrogance was based on the great British tradition that other people need rules, we don't. It is even more ridiculous that, having subsequently ceded the right to British citizens to bring cases at the European Court of Human Rights against their government, they are still not allowed to do the same in British courts. Those who petition Strasbourg spend many more years and many more thousands of pounds than they would if they could go to court here.

Following World War II, Britain helped draft a Convention on Human Rights it subsequently refused to incorporate into its own law. Such arrogance

The situation may be set to change with Lord Lester of Herne Hill's bill, introduced in the House of Lords, to incorporate the European Convention on Human Rights into British law. Similar bills have had majority support in the Lords in the past. If his bill does get to the Commons, it would bring real gains. Incorporation is the policy of both the Labour and Liberal Democrat parties and many individual Conservatives.

Lord Lester's bill would, for the first time, confer rights over and above what Parliament — with as little as a majority of one — chooses to grant us. These rights include freedom of expression and a fair trial. And while the bill does not allow for a mechanism that would overrule Parliament automatically if it contravened the Convention, it would offer more safeguards than we have at present.

But there needs to be a wider debate about rights generally. Charter 88's 'Citizens' Enquiry' into how we are governed, launched early this year, concentrates on rights as a key area for debate. The Enquiry will ask as wide a range of people as possible — what rights do you want? Do you want to go further than the European Convention that currently says nothing specific about the rights of gay men and lesbians not to be discriminated against? Or people with disabilities? Nor is the European Convention very specific about the rights of ethnic minorities: what would you want to add on immigration controls or religious policy? Would a Bill of Rights make any difference to the lives of black people in Britain? Or should the legal changes necessary be introduced via statute law? In Northern Ireland people from both the unionist and nationalist sides are talking about how a Bill of Rights could prevent religious discrimination in a future constitutional settlement. John Major is actively encouraging the discussion but says it would not be appropriate for England, Scotland or Wales. Why not? Is the government's stand on this defensible and will a Bill of Rights in Northern Ireland lead to inexorable pressure to have one elsewhere?

The debate must be underpinned by a popular discussion on whether people want to cling to or abandon the British doctrine of parliamentary sovereignty. If they want a Bill of Rights then how do they want to enforce it? With a US-style Supreme Court? How should its judges be chosen? Does reform of the judiciary need to come first and, if so, should there be a Judicial Appointments Commission and should there be better training of the judges? Should the court contain lay representatives? Should there be some halfway house where a court can ask Parliament not to pass laws that contravene a Bill of Rights, but where it does not have the power to declare Acts illegal? And how should the Bill of Rights be changed? By a majority of two thirds of members of Parliament or by referendum?

Charter 88 invites responses from people with all levels of expertise: from groups with legal expertise in fighting discrimination, from informal discussions held by people in their workplace or communities, and from individuals. We will present the findings to a cross-party panel of politicians in November this year as well as getting selected contributions published in the media. We aim to have any final consensus ready in March 1996. ❑

Leaflets on the Citizens' Enquiry, project pack order forms and a project pack on rights are available from The Citizens' Enquiry, Charter 88, Exmouth House, 3-11 Pine Street, London EC1R OJH, tel 0171 833 1988. Personal views or anything relevant already written should be sent to the same address

TERESA HAYTER

Repel all borders

The Single European Act provided for the free movement of goods, services, people and capital within Europe by January 1993. Only now and belatedly, does the EU plan to remove the 'final frontier', that which denies the free movement of people.

Charles Wardle, however, sacked from his job as immigration minister at the Home Office for poor presentation of government polices, is campaigning for the retention and even stricter enforcement of separate British border controls. He claims that EU borders are inadequately policed and that too many refugees and others from eastern Europe, Turkey, North Africa and elsewhere, having reached Germany and other more prosperous European countries, might choose to travel on to Britain (where unemployment is higher and wages and living conditions worse). Not only has Wardle been assured by Prime Minister John Major that Britain will retain its 'fair but firm' border controls; his arguments have also been backed by the shadow home secretary Jack Straw.

There is blatant inconsistency between Tory support for the removal of barriers to the free flow of goods within Europe and the desire to control the free movement of people. The government favours labour market flexibility within, but not between, countries. Consistency would demand that it welcome a bigger pool of labour to assist employers in disciplining their existing workforce — much as some have openly welcomed unemployment. Within the framework of free market economics, there is no rationale for immigration controls. They almost certainly have a marginal effect on the numbers entering Britain and are based on, and pander to, racist prejudice.

Controls are now used overwhelmingly against black people, a situation which was formalised in the 1981 legislation on 'patrials' and 'non-patrials' — those who do or do not have a British ancestor. The frequent claim that immigration controls are necessary for the sake of good race relations within Britain cannot be taken seriously. On the contrary, they fuel racism and xenophobia, giving them respectability and the seal of government approval. They give credence to ignorant scaremongering about the numbers of black people who live in this country or might wish to do so; their existence divides the working class and sets up black people as scapegoats for unemployment and the worsening economic conditions that are the product of the booms and slumps endemic to capitalism.

Britain's treatment of refugees and especially its detention policy, is among the worst in Europe. It was one of the first European countries to detain refugees and it is among the few that do so without trial or judicial safeguards.

Although all European countries now treat refugees with increasing harshness, in most of them the numbers of refugees are far larger in proportion to their populations than they are in Britain. The British share of refugees in the world as a whole is .015 per cent.

Immigration controls are a twentieth century invention. From the time the 1905 Nationalities Act was introduced to exclude Jews fleeing from pogroms in Russia and eastern Europe, the twentieth century history of British immigration controls has been a shameful one. Jews and other opponents of Hitler were interned during World War II; from 1962 onwards, black people from former British colonies were subjected to mounting restrictions. Today it is hard for them to come to Britain as visitors, let alone to settle and work. Even those who have lived and worked here for many years are increasingly likely to be arrested on some minor pretext and then have their immigration status checked. They may then find themselves, together with refugees, detained in prisons like Campsfield House, without trial, for indefinite periods.

Immigration controls have given rise to much suffering and many abuses. They have spawned a repressive and largely unaccountable apparatus of enforcement, of which the treatment of refugees is currently a particularly vicious manifestation. That neither the Tories nor, it seems, the Labour Party can accept even the limited freedom of movement proposed by the European Union, is a manifestation of the extent to which basic human rights and liberty are under threat in Britain. ❑

Total non-EU immigration 1992
(figures for Italy, Ireland & Austria not available)

DENMARK	25,238	⊗
BELGIUM	13,910	
FINLAND	8,979	
FRANCE	85,501	
GERMANY	1,066,508	
GREECE	10,132	
IRELAND	—	⊗
LUXEMBOURG	2,691	
NETHERLANDS	58,469	
PORTUGAL	11,852	
SPAIN	13,522	
SWEDEN	29,569	
UK	53,900	⊗

⊗ *Passport still required for travel to and from other EU countries*

EU countries
● *Passports must be shown at all borders when entering from outside the EU*
● *'Blue channels' exist at customs for EU citizens when returning from outside the Union*
● *The nine million immigrants already living in Europe may need visas to cross internal borders*

MAURICE FRANKEL

Public and private concerns

As public and private sectors impose gagging contracts on their employees, the need for whistleblowers grows. But who will protect their interests?

How do we discover what government, or companies, do not want to tell us? The obstacles are great: we have no Freedom of Information Act. MPs are constantly probing, but even their powers are strictly limited. And much of select committees' work involves following up stories broken by others, not themselves uncovering misdemeanours.

The first glimpse of the truth often comes from someone inside the organisation involved. It may be passed to the press, an MP, a pressure group or a regulatory agency. But however formidable these bodies' investigatory skills, that initial inside information is crucial.

Reactions to whistleblowers — whether they act anonymously or speak out openly — are often ambivalent. The person we consider has performed a heroic public service will, in other eyes, be betraying the trust of colleagues or the institution. Blowing the whistle may sometimes be the *wrong* thing to do; but when something is seriously wrong, when the public is put at risk, and when a conscientious employee has tried everything to remedy the matter from the inside, the issues become clearer. The overriding public interest may lie in protecting our right to be told, and the whistleblower's right not to be punished for telling us. In a long series of cases under the civil law of confidence, the courts have acknowledged that the public interest sometimes requires the disclosure of confidential information. When the *Spycatcher* case reached the House of Lords, Lord Griffiths ruled: 'theoretically, if a member of the [security] service discovered that some iniquitous course of action was being pursued that was clearly detrimental to our national interest, and he was unable to persuade any senior member of his service or any member of the establishment, or the police, to do anything about it, then he should be relieved of his duty of confidence so that he could alert his fellow citizens to the impending danger.'

Yet even in such cases, where the law may uphold the right to publish, it frequently does not protect the discloser from reprisals. Neither government nor the private sector finds it easy to tolerate those who speak out of turn. They are likely to be dismissed, or even prosecuted, however serious the abuse they reveal.

When the new Official Secrets Act was introduced in 1989, ministers resolutely rejected a public interest defence to allow the civil servant who may have released information, or the journalist who published it, to defend themselves on the grounds that the disclosure was justified.

The then home secretary, Douglas Hurd, repeatedly claimed that such a defence was without precedent in the criminal law. In fact, the precedents not only exist but are found in the Home Office's own legislation — notably the obscenity laws, which contain precisely such a 'public good' defence.

The statute books are peppered with some 400 additional legal penalties for disclosing information. Many protect individual privacy but others criminalise officials for daring to disclose even safety information on dangerous products. Again, no public interest defence is available.

The contracts of both public and private sector employees [recently and most notably in the National Health Service and in academic institutions] increasingly contain gagging clauses, making the unauthorised disclosure of *any* information to *anyone* a disciplinary offence that could lead to dismissal.

Equally worrying is the trend for confidentiality clauses in out-of-court settlements. The victims of unfair dismissal, sex discrimination or dangerous consumer products may get their compensation — but only in return for a binding promise of silence. This may protect a negligent company's reputation. It also allows it to buy off the strongest claimants, undermining others by denying them the previous evidence.

Journalists sometimes risk imprisonment to protect their sources' anonymity — a basic requirement if those with evidence of wrongdoing are to come forward. Here the government operates a curious double standard. The legislation which allows us to see official information, from the Data Protection Act to the law opening up council meetings, all permit public authorities to conceal the identity of *their* sources. A similar principle applies during legal proceedings, where the identity of certain kinds of informants is often protected by public interest immunity certificates.

But when *journalists* argue that their sources too should be protected, the rules change. The Contempt of Court Act appears to allow journalists to protect sources in most cases. But it was shown to be near useless when, in 1990, journalist Bill Goodwin was held to be in contempt by the House of Lords for protecting his informant from a company who wanted it for no higher purpose than to punish the discloser and plug the leak.

Could whistleblowing ever be rendered unnecessary? A powerful Freedom of Information Act — which would expose information without the need for leaking — would help, but could never be more than a partial solution. Users would have to specify what they wanted to know. But where there is no reason to suspect something is amiss, no-one may bother to ask. Another approach is to help potential whistleblowers pursue their concerns more effectively internally. A new charity, Public Concern at Work*, provides legal and practical advice to concerned employees. It has already shown that it is able to help many employees raise concerns about misconduct within the organisation, sometimes having the problems remedied without publicity — or the victimisation that invariably follows.

But other measures are needed to enable genuine public interest disclosures to be made without fear of reprisals. This may require new statutory protection for whistleblowers, to ensure that those who have taken reasonable steps internally to deal with real concerns are not penalised if further disclosure is needed. It may take the threat of fines or damages against employers who victimise, to prevent the too common response, of shooting the messenger — and ignoring the problem. ❑

* *Public Concern at Work, tel: 0171 404 6609*
The forthcoming issue of the British Medical Journal *will include a survey of secrecy in the National Health Service*

AKTER HUSSEIN

Who needs racism?

Racism. Who needs it?
I don't need it. You don't need it.
So why have it?
Is it honestly worth it?

Why kill someone if they are black or Asian?
Do they really deserve to die?
What have they done wrong?
Oh I get it you wanna be a big tuff guy!

Swearing at someone in the street,
Does that make you feel alright?
Darbing graffiti on walls,
Will you sleep better at night?

What's the BNP and NF anyway?
A racist group I hear,
Why not join the Black and White Unite?
Then you'll have nothing to fear!

If you came to our land,
We wouldn't say No Whites!
We'd show you all the beautiful Scenery,
And all the beautiful sites.

If you were in my shoes,
You'd know how I feel,
Shall we be friends?
Is that a deal?

But somehow I think not,
It'll never work out,
Because I'll grow up as a man,
You'll stay as a lout!!!

PHIL MAXWELL/CAMERA PRESS

BY AKTER.H.

GERRY ADAMS

PETER CLARKE

Speaking of peace

Of all people it was Margaret Thatcher who, during a visit to Poland said: 'In modern societies, success depends on openness and free discussions. Suppress those things and you are unable to respond to the need for change.'

On the same day, 19 October 1988, the British government introduced censorship restrictions on Sinn Féin, thereby obstructing the very kind of free and open debate required to inform and influence British public and political opinion on the need for fundamental change in Ireland.

Consider how much further along the road to an agreed Ireland we might have been without censorship and media misinformation clouding the issues all these years.

There is a perception in Britain that censorship only came into effect in 1988 and that the lifting of the restrictions on Sinn Féin towards the end of last year now means that censorship is a dead duck, a thing of the past.

I wish, at this most crucial stage in the evolving peace process, that this were true. But it is not. One cannot legislate for censorship restrictions to end one day and the following day expect British journalists and broadcasting corporations to miraculously rectify the imbalance created by decades of biased reporting.

Indeed, it could be argued that irresponsible and often mischievous reporting contributed to the conflict and, on occasions, influenced loyalist paramilitaries, the British army and Royal Ulster Constabulary (RUC) to harass and target our members and supporters.

It would be totally unrealistic to expect that such conditioning and prejudice directed against republicans — to the extent that it became institutionalised — would automatically shift into neutral. What has happened is that a sea change of expectation and hope for lasting peace has been created in the hearts and minds of the vast majority of people on these islands. They expect nothing less than the exploration of every possible opportunity and every possible avenue to consolidate the peace that now exists.

At this decisive watershed in our mutual histories there has never been a stronger feeling among so many on these islands that this process should neither be obstructed nor squandered: not by the two governments, not by any of the political parties, the media or any other party to the conflict.

I urge the British media, which has an awesome responsibility in the overall peace process, to meet the challenge of this new era in Anglo-Irish relationships by establishing a truly free and open press.

A positive move in this direction would be the immediate ending of the current restrictions placed on Sinn Féin spokespersons by the broadcasting media during studio discussions and interviews. The current

January 1994: the government of the Irish Republic abolishes Section 31 of its Broadcasting Act, the equivalent of the Hurd ban on broadcasting the voices of IRA and Sinn Féin members in the UK remained.
February: the ban is 'exported'. CNN, uplinked from London to the Astra satellite and thus subject to UK broadcasting regulations, is unable to show its viewers in Europe, the Middle East and Africa a live transmission of Gerry Adams being interviewed for an hour on Larry King Live. It has to be dubbed and goes out 12 hours after the event. (Shortly after, CNN switches its uplink to Luxembourg.) A similar fate befalls the Today Show on NBC Super Channel, uplinked from London to Eutelsat 2 Fl.
May: the European Court of Human Rights rules an application to challenge the ban by seven broadcasters and journalists and a member of the public inadmissible.
September: The Hurd ban is lifted in response to the IRA ceasefire. JP

situation is that broadcasters are bowing — perhaps not too reluctantly it must be said — to unionist demands that Sinn Féin spokespersons are interviewed separately from them. If this is not adhered to, unionists have threatened to withdraw from the debate.

Why should Sinn Féin be expected to comply with this arrangement? We are not issuing threats and laying down preconditions! Is it not the business of the broadcasting media to provide a level playing pitch for debate, and up to those invited to

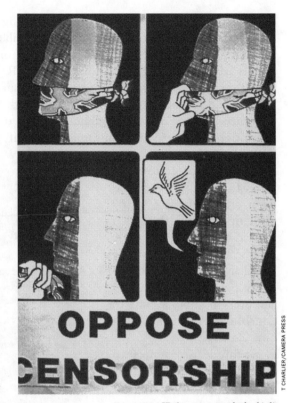

IRA poster: watch the birdie

engage or not engage? Such an open-door approach would contribute significantly to the peace process. It is, after all, inevitable that we will all be talking to each other to map out our future.

There is a perception that the British government's removal of the broadcast restrictions is evidence of its commitment to the peace process. While this view does not stand up to serious scrutiny, Sinn Féin was among the many political, human rights organisations and others to welcome the government's decision to end the ban and it is important that people, especially in Britain, understand why the ban was eventually lifted.

From its inception the ban presented the government with many headaches as it tried to justify the unjustifiable. Censorship, after all, is regarded as a tool of dictatorships, not 'democratic governments'.

The controversy surrounding the broadcast restrictions was brought to a head, in my view, by my visit to the USA in February 1994. The US media made much of their ability to carry the voice of 'the man whose voice is banned in Britain'. It was a serious embarrassment for the British government and in the weeks and months following that brief visit, the existence of censorship placed a serious question mark over its commitment to the peace process.

But we are still a long way from the situation where the peace debate can be conducted in a climate of openness and free discussion. The media bears a heavy responsibility for shaping and influencing events. As the peace process moves into the next phase of all-party talks, I would like to believe that it will carry out this function, by righting the wrongs of the past and accommodating developments in a climate of openness. ❑

CHARLES GLASS

Made in Heaven, banned in Britain

The book *Jeff Koons*, published by the German firm Taschen in 1992, is still in print, sold in many British book shops. The large format paperback is a catalogue of Koons's various works of art, presented in sections that represent successive periods of the young American's productive life. Beginning in 1979 with a mounted coffee pot and a vacuum cleaner, it moves through his years' designing advertisements for cigarettes, whisky and tennis shoes, then to the baroque and Disney-like figurines of his 'Banality' show in 1988. The penultimate section, 'Made in Heaven', includes several oil inks on canvas that look like photographs in lurid colour.

The pictures show the artist making love to his then wife, Ilona Staller, better known as the blonde former Italian parliamentarian and pornographic film actress La Cicciolina. In many of these portraits of the two lovers, Koons's uncircumcised penis is exposed and at full length. In some, his penis is in Ilona's mouth, in another in her vagina and in one, 'Red Butt (Close-Up), 1991', in her anus, while Ilona's own fingers are rubbing her clitoris. In others, his penis is spewing semen on his wife's mouth and legs.

Photographs of the type are sold legally in most European countries, from Spain to Germany, but not in Britain. Here, they are considered pornographic and are illegal.

Geoffrey Robertson, QC, writes in his *Freedom, the Individual and the Law* (Penguin 1993), that under the 1959 Obscene Publications Act 'DPP and Crown Prosecution Service officials have their lines to draw and they draw them fairly consistently at the male groin: nudity is now acceptable and even artistic, but to erect a penis is to provoke prosecution.' Yet the Koons book avoided prosecution, while magazines from Scandinavia and Thailand have not.

When *Jeff Koons* first appeared in Britain, to coincide with an exhibition of Koons's work, it was sold in shrink wrappers with a warning that the book contained material that some might consider obscene. It was a rare act of generosity on the part of HM Customs to admit the book into the country at all. They may have been persuaded to make an exception to their usual policy of seizing anything that depicted an erect penis, copulation or cunnilingus by the child-proof covering, the learned article on Koons the artist, the long interview Koons gave to the journalist Anthony Haden-Guest and the fact that a majority of the book's pictures are non-sexual.

Three years after publication, *Jeff Koons* is sold openly in bookshops without any covering or warning. Nothing remarkable about that, but for those erect penises, the penetrations and semen, which are prohibited in the 'Adults Only' bookshops of Soho.

It has, however, been censored — up to a point. At branches of the discount chain, Book Warehouse, all the photographs of Koons erect and the Koons-Staller insertions have the relevant portions blacked over. The blacking was not done by hand in ink, but by the publishers themselves on their presses. The censored pictures are faintly ridiculous. What would someone who had not seen the original imagine Ilona was holding in her

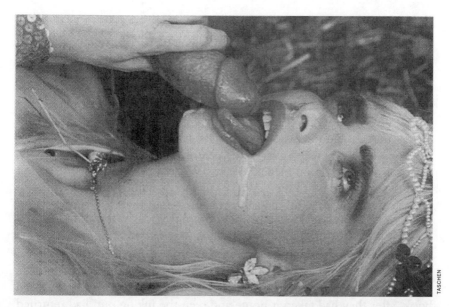

Made in Heaven: this could be art...

...but this is definitely pornography

hand as Jeff throws his head back in apparent ecstasy? What is it Jeff is licking as Ilona opens her mouth in what may be a sigh? Where did the white liquid around Ilona's mouth originate if not from the strange black box over her head? The censorship is all the more absurd when there are photographs of Koons' companion masterpieces on the same pages: life-size plasticine statues and glass figurines of Mr and Mrs Koons in the same and even more inventive *Kama Sutra* positions. What one can see in plastic and glass, one cannot see in ink on canvas or in photographs. If any book has ever made an ass of the censor, this is it.

Koons told Anthony Haden-Guest: 'What I tried to do is use myself as an example and go to the depths of hypocrisy and come back up — to resurface without making any direct moral judgements. The art world uses taste as a form of segregation.' The hypocrisy is there, not in the book so much as in British law on obscenity.

Book Warehouse said they sold the uncensored version at first, but the current stock with black boxes over the genitalia came directly from the publishers in Cologne. They added that many buyers of the censored book, after they had taken it home and seen the inking out, had returned it. No one had returned the uncensored version. 'The censored one doesn't sell as well,' a spokesman for Book Warehouse said. A spokeswoman at the publisher's Cologne headquarters said the black boxes had been superimposed for sale in Japan. She was surprised to learn they were in Britain.

The existence of two versions of the Koons book and the prohibition against the sale of explicit sex in pornographic magazines stems from legal distinctions in the Obscene Publications Act of 1959. The Act, in Robertson's words, enshrines 'the simplistic notion that sexual material could be divided into two classes, "literature" and "pornography"'.

Someone decided the Koons book was 'literature' and that downmarket magazines showing exactly the same body parts and the same acts were 'pornography'. The first is legal, meant for the literati and the artsy crowd, while the latter, intended for the masses, is illegal.

The Williams Committee recommendations (Report of the Committee on Obscenity and Film Censorship, 1979, HMSO 7772) recommended abolition of the distinction and proposed greater freedom of expression. No government has acted on the report, preferring the traditional politicians' response to pornography and most other things: hypocrisy. ❏

BEATRIX CAMPBELL

Moral panic

Things are never what they seem. The debate on video violence has been dramatically entered by protagonists who appear to be touching the nerves of common sense, but turn out to be defending something else

BFI STILLS, POSTERS AND DESIGNS

Child's Play 3: guilty?

The alliances for and against censorship have traditionally confounded conventional political alignments — misogynist moral re-armers and feminist critics of sexploitation find themselves in an unlikely coalition. Civil libertarian feminists join sceptical scholars in their critique of cause and effect: the notion that violent videos cause crime.

The pro-censors depend on a belief that there is a strong correlation between sex 'n' violence videos and criminal behaviour. If that correlation is secure, then censorship would control access — and effects.

The anti-censors depended on the absence of demonstrable cause and effect to support civil libertarian anti-statism.

What infused the temper of the debate was the horror revival as a tremendously popular genre, and the domestication of video technology.

If the victimisation of women animated the debate in the 1980s, in the 1990s children moved to the centre of public anxiety: children as the vulnerable, corruptible consumers.

Ironically, videos were then mobilised against children's evidence of their exploitation by adults; the corruptible child became the contaminated child, the killer child.

Class snobbery infused a moral panic: it was the deprived who were expected to be depraved.

The inflammatory effects of the abduction of two-year-old Jamie Bulger in 1994 transformed the debate both because a video nasty was cited in the case and because short-circuit surveillance video recorded an image of two boys taking the child from the Bootle mall where his mother was shopping.

The case ignited a new recruit to the censorship lobby, Professor Elizabeth Newson, who lent liberal credentials to the authoritarian Liberal Democrat MP David Alton's crusade against video nasties.

Reflecting on the critical response to her paper for Alton, published in *The Psychologist* in July 1994, she wrote that she had not considered that middle class 'children are at risk from the pornography of violence in the houses of their middle class friends'.

Professor Newson appears at the conjuncture between the campaign against horror video culture that expanded in the 1980s, and the crusade against children's evidence of abuse that dominated child protection controversies in the 1990s. She changed the terms of the conversation.

Although the pro-censors cannot demonstrate cause and effect, their resonance in common sense is fortified by real experience of sexual threat to women and children, and the proliferation of both public and personal violence in a post-Cold War world.

Their critics can demonstrate the absence of cause and effect but, oddly, their rigour is determinedly disconnected from what animates the sex 'n' violence discourse: a belief that the enjoyment of sex and violence endorses dangerousness.

But the Bulger case and Newson's intervention shifted the balance of sensibility. Saying very little, the boys themselves were never able to illuminate what or who made them murder baby Jamie. These questions were apparently answered by the video nasty, *Child's Play 3*, that drifted across the case, never quite settling anywhere.

The historian of censorship in the British film industry, Tom Dewe

Mathews, author of *Censored* (*Index* 4&5/1994), describes it as a vital moment, a 'classic case of symbolic politics'.

The footage of the shopping centre challenged an undoubted expectation of *adult* abductors. We would not have guessed that children took the child had we not seen it with our own eyes.

But what did we think we were seeing? The gritty videoed moment in the shopping mall was an instant. 'What we saw was a *still* video image, but we interpreted it as a *moving* image,' says Tom Dewe Mathews. That transformed not only what we knew about the abductors but what we could imagine about ourselves: 'We could put ourselves in the position of asking ourselves "what would I have done" because the murder had lots of points of possible intervention.'

That still from the shopping mall video became symbolically confused with fantasies about what might have motivated the children. A video! *Child's Play 3* drifted across the empty emotional landscape. The trial judge, Mr Justice Morland, speculated that perhaps these children had seen videos that provided a template that was then imitated in the child killers' *modus operandi*. He didn't know.

We don't know. But that didn't matter. It became fixed: *Child's Play 3* was to blame. It didn't matter that no-one knew whether they'd seen it, or that the video did not match their action. If anything provided a video link it would have been *The Railway Children*, commented the police investigator Alfred Kirkby.

Professor Elizabeth Newson, who is not known for academic research on either the impact of the media or on the abuse of children, provided an intellectual constituency — her paper acquired 25 signatories — for David Alton's amendments to the 1984 Video Recordings Amendment Act, which were ultimately assimilated into the Criminal Justice Bill with the support of Labour leader Tony Blair and Home Secretary Michael Howard.

Professor Newson's paper began with the Bulger case and what could have precipitated it. What is new in the lives of children? she asks. 'The easy availability to children of gross images of violence on video.'

This formula is the key to her participation in the movement to discredit children's accounts of sexual crimes perpetrated by adults, a movement that seems to prefer the notion of abuse by video to the evidence of abuse by adults.

Professor Newson's first role as an 'expert' in a child abuse controversy supported the belief that children — whose evidence led to the conviction of 10 adults for sex offences — could have been influenced by books or videos or brainwashing by their foster carers and social workers. The hypothesis offered by her and her husband John Newson endorsed the police in the Nottingham case in 1989, who had failed initially to investigate the children's allegations and then promised to discredit their evidence that orbiting around their parents were other adults interested in pornography, drugs and the occult.

It became conventional wisdom that these children had been brainwashed by carers or contaminated and confused by videos despite the fact that every High Court judge in half a dozen child protection proceedings in the Nottingham case concluded after contemplating all the evidence (including the brainwashing/video hypothesis) that the children had been abused in bizarre occult contexts by real, live adults.

In her Alton paper she invokes the other well-known child abuse controversy, the Rochdale case in 1990, in which allegations of ritual abuse of children were thrown out by Mr Justice Brown. An expert witness (not a social worker) for the Official Solicitor argued that the children, who had indeed watched horror videos, were able to distinguish between fact and fantasy, and were clear: their

Nightmare on Elm Street: guilty?

stories about videos described what they had seen, not what they had experienced. The judge was not convinced and was persuaded by Professor Newson and another expert witness, Valerie Mellor, that material from videos might have featured in their stories. 'Mr Justice Brown identified children's access to videos as cause for concern,' she wrote in her Alton paper. 'The children's familiarity with horror images from videos such as *Nightmare on Elm Street* misled social workers into assuming that they must have experienced such things in reality.'

Videos, apparently, explained alleged abuse away. Videos, it seemed, contaminated not only children but social workers; they appeared to explain children's fantasies, not their reality. They might incite children to commit crime (the Bulger killing), or cause social workers to imagine that crimes were being committed against children.

It was the case of Suzanne Capper, a young woman torched by a group of sadistic friends, that clinched Newson's case: Suzanne Capper's torturers had used the *Child's Play 3* video, she wrote. The terrifying case apparently gave Newson and the pro-censorship lobby what it wanted: the act of imitation.

She told the House of Commons Home Affairs Select Committee on 22 June 1994, when it interviewed witnesses on video violence, that 'there is enough evidence of imitation.' But the only evidence she could offer was the Capper case: 'The Suzanne Capper case is another example of a very explicit imitation of video and the use of video and that was *Child's Play 3*.'

But she was wrong. The committee informed her that, in fact, a radio rock version of the sound track was played while the young woman was tormented. Was music, rather than a tacky video, the culprit?

When she appeared before the committee she was not endorsed by the two other experts — one on videos and violence, the other on child abuse. Neither Dr Guy Cumberbatch, the premier British researcher on the impact of sex 'n' violence videos, nor the NSPCC, a major agency charged with child protection, supported either her imitation thesis or the correlation thesis forwarded by Newson and the pro-censorship lobby.

But what Profession Newson's passionate intervention demonstrated was the way the debate diverted attention away from adults: the new cause for concern was not the spectre of cruelty *to* children but the cruelty *of* children — as accusers or as killers infected by the video nasty. ❏

POSY SIMMONDS

CHRISTOPHER HIRD

In camera

At the beginning of this year at a private seminar in London for journalists, television producers and lawyers, one of the speakers articulated a view increasingly shared by people in British television. Investigative journalism, he said, was in a bad way in Britain. At the BBC there was a 'numbing bureaucracy'; ITV — Britain's main commercial channel — was now almost entirely ratings driven; and Channel 4 — once regarded as Britain's riskiest and most adventuresome television channel — was now working to a different agenda.

The speaker was an extremely experienced television producer who had made a wide range of factual programmes over a number of years. In his view 'the economic and commercial situation in our industry makes it hard to do investigative journalism.' With the term investigative journalism he was defining a wide range of journalism which, in the words of a former editor of the *New Statesman*, Bruce Page, is involved in 'exposing unwelcome facts, championing unpopular minorities and insisting against all pressure that the common people shall be informed of what uses and misuses are being made of their courage and virtue'. Something, in other words, which lies at the heart of the journalistic endeavour and a free media.

Britain appears to be a society with an enviably high standard of freedom of speech, reflected in its censor-free media. However, as the remarks of the speaker at the London seminar suggest, now may be the time to examine critically the received wisdom that Britain's media is free from censorship.

> When I did a TV series on BBC 2 in 1984 I wasn't allowed to say 'Lil-lets' — this year on BBC 1 I was! Hooray!
>
> *Victoria Wood*

Until the beginning of 1994 Britain had a highly regulated television industry. ITV was a privately-owned, profit-making, advertising-financed television channel but the parameters of what it could broadcast were tightly defined by the regulatory body and by the countervailing power of the BBC. At the same time Channel 4 — which has a statutory obligation to produce innovative programmes and serve viewers which the other channels don't — had a semi-protected status as it was financed by subventions from the ITV companies. In this delicate ecosystem of broadcasting Britain produced a remarkably diverse range of factual programming.

> Believe it or not, everything I've ever wanted to say on television I have found a way of saying and indeed have been encouraged to do so.
>
> *Ben Elton*

In 1994 a new system came into being. The cornerstone of this system was that the right to broadcast ITV programmes went to the highest bidder. In some cases companies had to make payments to the government of literally tens of millions of pounds every year just for the right to broadcast. At the same time, the regulatory grip on programmes was relaxed. The ITV companies had to drive for ratings, to provide a return for their shareholders. Difficult, enquiring factual programming slipped down the list of priorities.

Over at Channel 4 the company was allowed to compete directly for its own advertising and became a free-standing operation. At the BBC, more complicated changes had been underway. Under the leadership of John Birt the corporation had been fighting a battle with the government both to maintain its licence fee income and to stay in the public sector. Perhaps uniquely in the British public sector, this was a successful battle. However, many in the BBC believed that the price was a trimming of the sharper edge of the BBC's journalism — particularly in relation to coverage of politics and institutions of the state. This belief received powerful public endorsement earlier this year when Birt made a speech in which he was openly critical of the aggressive questioning to which many politicians were subjected by his own staff.

On 27 October 1994, The Big Story's 'Rich Man...Poor Man', contrasts consultancy-laden Tory MPs with low wage earners forced to moonlight on multiple jobs in order to make ends meet. Producers Twenty Twenty Vision ask David Mellor if they can 'spend some time with you on an average working day'. He refuses, is doorstepped by a film crew who film him being driven away from his house in a car, and complains to Paul Jackson, managing director of Carlton, that he has been made to look 'shifty and evasive'. Jackson assures him the footage will not be used. Twenty Twenty refuse to remove the footage; Carlton does the deed itself. The production team insist on their names being removed from the credits. By 1 November, at a meeting with Stuart Prebble, controller of factual programmes at the ITV Network Centre, Carlton admits it has been mistaken in insisting on the cut and gives an assurance that such a situation will not happen again. JP

Part also of the campaign to keep the BBC public was an increased concern to improve the ratings. This has certainly been one of the influences which has encouraged the growth of the fly-on-the-wall documentary. Whereas once the BBC might expose wrong-doing by the police or army, now its executives try and negotiate access to these institutions to make a series about their work. The critical attitude of the journalist is often replaced by the uncritical lens of the camera.

Together, these forces at work in broadcasting are liable to encourage in organisations a form of self-censorship, in which programme makers only offer up ideas which will accord with the predominant culture. This, of course, can apply in any organisation but, unfettered, the commercial imperative can be the most powerful influence in affecting the creative culture.

Against these somewhat pessimistic threads which can be drawn out of what is happening to the British media, there are a number of more optimistic ones. Market research shows that viewers and listeners want politicians to be held to account. On all Britain's television channels every week there are still programmes which investigate those areas of British public life which bureaucrats, business people, politicians and others would like kept quiet. And throughout broadcasting there are those committed to making and broadcasting such programmes. But the experience of the last few years has shown the fragility of the pluralistic culture which has characterised much of British broadcasting since the 1950s. The responsibility for maintaining and enriching this culture is in the hands of journalists and programme makers themselves — by keeping the debate going, by agitating to make the programmes they believe in and by transmitting those programmes. ❑

> I once heard a comic nego-tiating with a producer next door to me on *Friday Night Live*. Comic was say-ing: 'So if I drop "a wanker" can I have two "toffee bollocks?"'
> Producer agreed.
>
> *Jo Brand*

JULIAN PETLEY
Rag-bag regulation

With the proliferation of moral watch dogs, television is more censured than censored

The Jordache story: censured

There are now four bodies with the power to censure broadcasters — the Broadcasting Standards Council (BSC), the Broadcasting Complaints Commission (BCC), the Independent Television Commission (ITC), and the new BBC Programme Complaints Unit. Targets for censure in 1994/5 included:
Brookside (drug-taking), *Brookside* Special 'The Jordache Story' (too early, not enough warning of content); *Cutting Edge* 'Graham Taylor — the Impossible Job' (language); *Without Walls* 'Expletive Deleted' and 'The Greatest F★★★★★★ Show on Television' (guess); *Emmerdale* (violence, and a general trend towards sensationalism); *The Paul Daniels Magic Show* (an overly realistic — though faked — cremation of Debbie McGee); *The Word* (the inclusion of a 'grossly offensive' and 'wholly unacceptable' joke); *Panorama* 'Babies on Benefit' (misleading and unfair'); and *The Brief* ('unfair').

In November 1994 *Broadcast* magazine leaks details of an unpublished ITC survey, based on a comparison of two two-week 'snapshots' from 1993 and 1994 schedules, alleging that there has been an increase of 18 per cent and 33 per cent of violence in ITV and Channel 4 programmes respectively. The figures are rejected as crude, superficial and over-reliant on quantitative analysis by ITV and Channel 4 insiders; the ITC admits that no programme monitored had breached its programme code. Nevertheless, ITC director of programmes, Clare Mulholland, argues that the survey 'failed to produce evidence that the looked-for reduction in levels of violence has taken place', and notes that 'successive surveys have found that two-thirds of viewers continue to believe that there is too much violence on television.' Her views are echoed by the Heritage Department's statement that 'the government shares the public's concern and hopes the regulator's involvement will make the broadcasters responsive to the concerns of the audience.'

But in January 1994, the BCC's second Monitoring Report, based on a similar 'snapshot' of all terrestrial channels in 1992 and 1993 concludes that 'unacceptable language, unacceptable explicit sex and unacceptable violence were each reported as existing in only one per cent of programmes seen on terrestrial channels.'

At the Edinburgh Television Festival in August, Michael Grade attacks 'a clumsy patchwork of regulators stitched together in the last few years in response to the Mary Whitehouse tendency', and calls for the abolition of the 'goodie two-shoes, middle-class, middle-brow, narrow-minded and totally unrepresentative' BSC and BCC. It is unnecessary for ITV and Channel 4 to be regulated by 'three overlapping quangos tripping over each other touting for complaints business in order to justify their existence'. In Grade's view, the job of regulating all broadcasting should be left to the ITC.

The BBC is also in uncharacteristically bullish mood over censure when it decides to fight back over the BCC. In September, forced to broadcast the BCC's ruling on *Panorama*'s 'Babies on Benefit', the BBC adds its own denunciation of the BCC's actions and seeks judicial review on the grounds that the complainant to the BCC, the National Council for One Parent Families, was not directly involved in the original programme. In October Channel 4 launches a similar action against the BCC's ruling on *The Brief*. It loses, but is given leave to appeal. In February 1995 Mr Justice Brooke rules that the BCC has acted beyond its powers in the *Panorama* case, thereby banishing the spectre of partisan pressure groups lining up at the BCC's door with spurious protests about programmes in which they were never involved. The way is now open for Channel 4 to mount an appeal.

This is not *Panorama*'s only problem in 1994. In May an edition on the alleged 'gerrymandering' by Westminster Council is withdrawn because of problems with section 30 of the Local Government Act on the legality of quoting from an unpublished district auditor's report. The programme is eventually screened, but after (and not before, as planned) local council elections (in which the Tories manage to hang on to the 45 seats they are defending). In July 'Grassed', an edition on the changing role of police informants, is postponed after pressure from senior officers claim it could endanger the lives of informants. ❑

Babies on benefit

PAUL FOOT

PETER CLARKE

Enough is enough

In the middle of March last year, the Central Television programme *The Cook Report* and its famous presenter, Roger Cook, were sitting on one of the great journalistic scoops of modern times: a scoop that threatened to bring down the government.

In an ingenious 'sting' operation the programme's researchers set up a bogus company ostensibly selling priceless Russian works of art which they had commandeered during the collapse of Communism. In this guise, they approached the parliamentary lobbyists, Ian Greer Associates, and asked for help in purchasing a newly privatised government department, the Insolvency Agency, to help them gather information about British business. Greer and his minions responded with tremendous enthusiasm. In a series of secretly-filmed meetings, they promised to 'open the door' to the offices of influential people of all kinds, of senior ministers, even of the prime minister.

Just as these invaluable contacts were about to be delivered to the secret cameras, the programme was suddenly and inexplicably cancelled. The news was passed to the astonished Cook team by the managing director of Central TV, Andy Allan. Earlier that year, the fiercely independent Central had been swallowed by Carlton, the enormously powerful London company that had won the franchise from Thames Television after the latter had infuriated Prime Minister Thatcher by daring to tell the truth about the shooting of three unarmed IRA members in Gibraltar. Most journalists in Central at the time linked the blatant censorship of the programme with the take-over of their company by Carlton, and none of the lame excuses from the company — nor the recent half-baked attempts to get the unfinished, censored programme on the air — have suggested otherwise.

The old rules that governed the franchising of commercial televisions were devised primarily to prevent a concentration of ownership. It seemed obvious that if a handful of individuals got control of all commercial television, choice and diversity of programmes would suffer. So the franchises were divided into geographical units and safeguarded from take-over. Many of these careful rules have recently been swept aside. In a sudden burst of take-over activity, Carlton has swallowed Central, Granada LWT, Meridian Anglia.

The same drive to monopoly has been poisoning the press. When Rupert Murdoch moved his British newspaper publishing headquarters to Wapping in 1986 and smashed the trade union, optimists predicted a 'new age of diversity' for British newspapers. The 'restrictive influences' of trade unions and the old technology on which they thrived would be replaced by cheaper technology, cheaper labour — and, as a result, many, more diverse newspapers. Exactly the opposite happened. The three new national daily newspapers to have started and survived since 1986 — *Today* and the daily *Independent* and *Sunday Independent* — have been swallowed by the two biggest press monopolies — News International and the Mirror Group.

Exactly the same trend can be seen in cable television, radio and the local press. Even the conservative Monopolies Commission thought that diversity of opinion and news would be threatened by the take-over by the *Daily Mail* of the *Nottingham Evening Post*, and recommended against it. But the government, after imposing a few trivial and face-saving conditions, waved the new monopoly through. ITN, whose independence is still guaranteed by irrelevant and ignored statute, is now effectively owned by two men. All the gory details of the new media monopoly are set down with great force in the recent booklet by the

CENTRAL TV

Roger Cook

*O*n 12 May 1994 the Guardian *leads
on a story by its Westminster
correspondent David Hencke which reveals
that, the previous month, Central halted a*
Cook Report *investigation into Ian Greer
Associates, one of Britain's biggest political
lobbyists.*

*Although more than 50 MPs table a motion
inviting the Commons Members' Interests
and Privileges Committee to order Central to
make the film available to a Commons
enquiry into lobbying activities, nothing
happens. Central always maintained that
this edition was dropped because 'this story
did not come up to scratch' and that 'it did
not make a Cook programme.' It refuses to
screen any material for MPs because 'it is not
Central's policy to disclose untransmitted
material.'*

*Greer Associates has acted for Carlton, which
merged with Central early in 1994 and
which shares Andy Allan as its chief
executive. Greer Associates also provides a
monitoring service on Commons broadcasting
matters to the ITV Association, which is
chaired by Leslie Hill, also chair of Central
and a member of the Carlton Board. JP*

Campaign for Press and
Broadcasting Freedom —
*Britain's Media — How they are
Related.**

Now, under pressure from
one of the most powerful
pressure groups ever formed,
the British Media Group, the
government is preparing to
sweep away almost all the
remaining safeguards against
media monopoly. The British
Media Group was formed in
July 1993 by Associated
Newspapers (the *Daily Mail*
etc), Pearson (*The Financial
Times* etc), the freedom-
loving Guardian group and
the *Telegraph*. Its aim is to
allow the big media groups to
buy more and more
television, radio and
newspapers and to turn what
is already a highly
concentrated industry into a
full-blown monopoly.

Does this matter? Surely
owners are necessary to keep
papers going — and are they
not neutral observers who do
not interfere with or restrict
their editors? Anyone who
has ever worked for any of the
increasingly monopolised
media will be ready with the
answer. The tycoons' control
is not remote. It creeps down,
and pervasively, onto the

editorial floors and the production studios. The owners appoint their editors, the editors their deputies and executives, in their own image. Promotion and success depend on pleasing the owners and their appointees. The owners are not neutral. They are keen propagandists with a determined political agenda. Lord Stevens, as fine a representative of the new breed of owners as his former friend and associate Robert Maxwell, has summed up his approach with typical aplomb: 'I do interfere and say "enough is enough". I don't ram my views in, but I'm quite far out to the right'. So are his newspapers, the *Express* and the *Star* plus countless local papers all over the country.

They are all, by the way, strong supporters of freedom and free media — free that is for their proprietors to own; and print, broadcast and censor exactly as they please. ❏

*Granville Williams Britain's Media — How they are Related: Media Ownership and Democracy *(CPBF, 1994)*

GODFREY HODGSON

A matter of prejudice

The British press, the feisty editor of the *Sunday Times*, Harold Evans, used to say 25 years ago, is half-free. He meant that, although we have little formal censorship, a whole web of constraints inhibits British newspapers from publishing news the readers ought to know. But today, the nature of those constraints has changed.

In 1967, when I went to work for Evans as the editor of 'Insight', then the *Sunday Times'* investigative team, the main threats came from libel (we were repeatedly sued by Robert Maxwell, and never lost an action); from the general climate of secretiveness; and from the paranoid secrecy of government in general and the Secret Intelligence Service in particular.

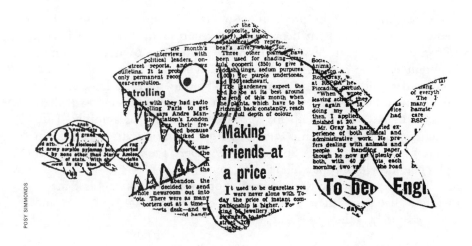

POSY SIMMONDS

We did not complain about the libel law as such but we did feel we were unreasonably obstructed by the way the legal system worked. There were (probably still are) oppressive rules: for example, when after mountainous research we found an instance where Maxwell had signed two affidavits on the same day, one (when he was borrowing money) swearing that he was broke, we could not introduce the affidavits as evidence of fraud unless we could produce the notary public before whom they had been sworn...and he turned out to have been hired by Maxwell!

The general climate of secretiveness struck me because I had previously been working in the United States, where a 'First Amendment culture' produces a prima facie assumption that the media have a right to be informed, even if they are then disinformed. Civil servants, businessmen and ordinary people who had access to information of public importance seemed to feel absolutely no obligation to make it public.

Cold War paranoia is hard to imagine now. Many British journalists, especially foreign correspondents, were in one form of relationship with the secret services or another. On one occasion the proofs of a carefully researched report on British involvement in the civil war in the Yemen were stolen from my office and appeared the next day in the *Daily Telegraph* virtually unchanged except for an intro saying, in effect: 'The following lies are being circulated by anti-British circles in Cairo.'

Libel, government secrecy and the general climate still inhibit serious journalism in Britain, but less than they did 25 years ago. The 'D notice' system of self-censorship is in abeyance, and the Thatcher government overplayed its hand so badly in the Ponting case that the Official Secrets Act, too, is less of a threat. Libel is still a problem, all the more so because the popular press is now so disreputable that courts award even heavier libel damages than they used to.

Other pressures, however, have greatly increased. One is pervasive commercial presure. Newspapers are less willing to devote time, space, money and manpower to getting to the bottom of what really happened. One of the most serious of recent national editors once asked me to write a profile of a political figure. I said I would need time to talk to the subject and a few people who knew him. 'Oh' said the editor, 'I didn't mean a researched profile!' Few newspapers now even attempt the kind of serious investigative effort we put into our reporting on — for example — Philby, thalidomide, Maxwell or improper interrogations in Northern Ireland.

Even worse is the pressure, direct and indirect, from proprietors. It is not, so far as I can tell, that Rupert Murdoch and Conrad Black often intervene to order their papers to take a certain line. It is rather that executives and editors anxious to please them recruit key staff from a narrow band of ideological persuasions, and conduct the kind of journalistic campaigns they imagine the boss will like. The first time in history, I imagine, that *The Times* wrote five leaders in a few days on a single subject was when it was campaigning against the BBC in the middle 1980s. The leaderwriter who decided to write those leaders, and he has assured me it was his own idea, rose with exceptional rapidity to become editor. Rupert Murdoch's editors pander to his imagined prejudices, against the monarchy, the BBC and the English upper-middle class. Conrad Black's prejudices are different ones, but the *Sunday Telegraph*, in particular, panders to them. He did, after all, announce when buying the *Telegraph* papers that one of his motives was to give President Reagan a more favourable press in Britain. His papers in London reflect a conservative bias in a way that would be inadmissible for a serious newspaper in the United States. We are daily reminded by the British press's coverage of Europe that seven of our dozen national daily and Sunday newspapers are owned by two ultra-conservative non-European proprietors. ❏

BABEL

Continuing our series focusing on the voices of those silenced by poverty, prejudice and exclusion

PENELOPE FARMER

Grenada calling

Diane, *a district nurse, came to Britain in 1966 aged 15; her daughter* Tami *was born here in 1972.* Sylvia *preceded her in 1959 'for five years' but trained as an auxiliary nurse and stayed on.* Kathy *arrived in 1965 'to better my way, to work, because I am always very poor. Working — cleaning — is what I am doing up till now';* her niece Ann *arrived when she was 12.* Anne *came in 1961: 'It was 12 April and not so cold. My boyfriend is here before me. I could not understand the way people were.' She, too, works as a domestic and contract cleaner. All the women are from Grenada*

Diane When I first came I got the impression all the houses were factories. It was October, so all the houses had smoke. And I'd never seen houses with basements before, and someone said 'what will your mother think of you living under somebody's house?'

Sylvia People were all right but it was winter then. When I got up and had to go out in the snow, I cry — I say I'm not going. After, I get used to it and I manage...

I always remember my first patient. Whenever you touch her she used to pinch and rub herself, she thought the black hands was going to remain on her. But you get over it. It was a job I was doing — I didn't meet any problems like racism. But I know it's there.

Kathy Sometimes on a bus they call you names. But I don't take any notice. I just carry on.

Tami Back in the West Indies, I see every different type and mix; black and Indian; black and white; black and Chinese. But I just see them as Grenadians, Trinidadians, whatever. But over here, someone mixes, black and Chinese are called a 'ching', someone black and Indian a 'dougla'; and when they don't know the mixture, they'll call them 'mulatto' or something like that. Which I find really racist. They're putting labels on people.

Anne I live in my street for 19 years. And there's an Indian house next door to me, and people there they never say hullo to me, and I never say hullo to them. They just don't like black people.

Tami At the end of the day — and I feel bad saying this — the worst barrier of racism is within our own race. The Barbadians, the Jamaicans in particular, they're really funny about light skin and dark skin.

Diane I went to Barbados in 'sixty-something on a school exchange scheme, and even in church they have this problem, you can't commune at the same time with someone white or light-skinned; there were some university students

Britain 1950s: first arrivals

The Nurse-wife's tale

We was married in 1960 — on the 31st of December. I'd been here a year then. Before I left my mother she said to me: 'Wherever you go there is fire; there is water; there is earth. So when you are in England don't bother to send anything home — they know you're there and there's always water to bathe and fire to cook. And always remember, respect the law of the land.' And I've always tried to.

I already had two children by Frank when I came. He didn't behave himself even then, back home in Grenada, but he promised my dad he'd marry me, and he did. We stayed married for 33 years till he died. And I went into auxiliary nursing and I stayed for 32 years. I would have liked to have more qualifications, but I had six children and a not very supportive husband, so I couldn't study for them. And I don't regret my work. I got a pension.

Things have changed here. In the West Indies it was the man's duty to go out and work. And the women did what the men wanted. But now the women stand up for themselves. The men used to say you must have all the children. But now the women say no.

[Our] men never settle down — they have children here, there, everywhere, sometimes girlfriends only a few doors away. Women don't accept that any more. They don't want husbands. They want children on their own.

My husband at least never had children outside. What I couldn't take was when his girlfriends started phoning home. Then I wanted to divorce. I kept hoping that things would change. Why I was holding on I don't know. I had to really struggle.

I can't think of any husband I know that doesn't treat his wife badly. My daughters' boyfriends treat them terrible. Three of them prefer to be by themselves — even the two that had children, because of the bad treatment. And the eldest one, she's in two minds whether to leave her husband.

One problem may be, though, is our women doing better than men at work. Men don't like it. They see black women working harder, trying to be independent because of the way men treat them. They say to the women: 'You're not going to kick me down.' In one way I'm lucky. He only ever hit me once. I remember my father beating my mother for no reason at all. And the beating still goes on. My daughter left her daughter's father because of that.

I had to stop working eventually because I had osteoarthritis. And then Frank's brother died and he never got over it. He became an alcoholic. All the time he was ill, he'd go crazy. I kept wishing he was dead. They'd take him into hospital for a while, I'd hope he'd die there. But he was very strong, he'd come home, and start drinking again. And then one morning I found him dead in bed.

I missed him, though. I felt bad because I'd wished he was dead. I'd like a man to go out with, do things with, but I'd never get married or live with a man again. I know what men are like. ❏

from one of the African countries and they had a lot of problems.

Tami But the Jamaicans…the prejudice is the other way about. I've experienced…like, a whole group of dark-skin girls coming to me and saying they were going to slice my face up —

Diane — because she's a half-caste —

Tami — and it looked bad, especially when the police came. You're all supposed to be one race black people, but it's dark-skinned girls, against one light-skinned girl. To the other kids, teachers, of course you're just black.

Ann When I came here in 1967, the education system was anti black children. My school was racist from the teachers down to the children. Though I applied and passed the entrance exam for college, the school wrote the reference saying that I wasn't reliable, you know, so they turned me down.

Tami My school was all right. It was the white side of their families the black kids had a problem with. Some of their daughters went out and got black boyfriends as a rebellion and dibbled and dabbled with them. Some of them got pregnant very young. One guy I know — his mum is white, his dad is black — suffered a lot because the white side of the family called him 'wog', 'nigger' to his face. It was the black side of the family helped see her through college and so on. And then she married a white guy, a racist. He was in the building trade — he'd make the little boy work for everything he got. He still suffers for it. He's always going to have a problem with white people.

Anne My eldest son, when he was out of work — his wife's white, and her parents run a pub outside London — her father say bring him down here, he can help run the pub. But his wife said: 'I'm sorry, dad, I won't bring him down there, they will call him too many names. I love him too much. He'll get hurt.'

Tami I don't mind too much. But some of my friends, they feel about it. They lash out — but my mum says, let it just bounce off. I think that's

JUDITH VIDAL-HALL

Ann: 'I've never felt England was my home'

the better way to handle it. You don't fight fire with fire. Racism went down when people of different cultures first started mixing. But it's rising again.

Diane In east London there's a big problem with Somalians. It's repeating itself like when West Indians were coming here. White people were thinking black people were coming here and taking apples from their mouths. Now West Indian people are feeling refugees are coming here and getting everything — and they who are born here, working here, not getting what they're entitled to.

Sylvia I said to someone the other day, now I know how white people felt when we were coming in, the West Indians. I'm totally against these Somalians coming here.

Tami They're really arrogant.

Diane I grew up being taught Britain is the mother country — I owe allegiance to Britain, Britain owes allegiance to me — but in my opinion and from the history and geography I know, Britain doesn't owe any allegiance to Somalians and they haven't done anything for Britain, they haven't contributed anything.

Tami The West Indians and the Somalians and the Arabs too — you say we're all a black race, and we should all get together. But at the end of the day, Africans hate West Indians. They say we ran away from them when we were put in ships — it's ridiculous the way they carry on.

Diane I say I'm black. Sylvia is black. Kathy and Anne, we are from the same island — but we have the family tree and our family history a long way back. But someone here in England wants to tell me that I am from Africa. But I say what part of Africa? It's nonsense. My great-great-grandfather was a Welshman — should I hold on to that, too? I'm not Afro-Caribbean, either. I hate to be classified like that.

Tami At school you've got certain teachers that ask you to write about how you feel coming from West Indian origin, or African origin. Then they say you're not angry enough. You're not showing the years of slavery — but at the end of the day if it doesn't affect you, if your forefathers didn't complain, I don't see why you should, you're not the ones suffering from it. We're living in the future, not going into the past.

Anne What I want is to go back to the West Indies. I feel I've had enough here.

Diane I'm the same. I've been here so long.

Sylvia When I'm here I want to go home and live in the West Indies. When I'm in the West Indies I want to go home to England. I don't know where is my home any more.

Anne A lot of older ones, who were here before us, they all went back.

Diane If you just live for the day, you get stuck. But Anne says she's going, Sylvia says she will, and Kathy. All of us are making plans.

Ann I've never been rooted. I've never felt like England's my home. I'd like to retire to Grenada as soon as possible. Financially I'm totally broken. But I still want one day to go home. ❏

INDEX ON CENSORSHIP

The important issues of the day.
Issues that you cannot afford to miss.

Tolerance (Issue 1-2/1994)

The relaunch issue: Umberto Eco, Salman Rushdie, Ronald Dworkin, Stephen Spender, James Fenton, Dubravka Ugresic, Anne Nelson and a special report on Egypt.

Liberty (Issue 3/1994)

Noam Chomsky on the US's foreign policy and Vaclav Havel on post-Communist life. Plus Bob Sutcliffe, Shada Islam and Isabelle Ligner on the contentious matter of immigration.

Media (Issue 4-5/1994)

Christopher Hird, Ted Turner, Clive Hollick and Matthew Hoffman on the concentration of media ownership. European writers—A S Byatt, Bora Cosic and Julian Barnes—pay tribute to Sarajevo.

Intervention (Issue 6/1994)

Humanitarian aid as the latest form of intervention: Alex de Waal in Africa, Jane Regan in Haiti, Julie Flint in Iraq. The turbulent years since the Velvet Revolution: W L Webb, Ivan Klima and Ryszard Kapuscinski.

Gay's the word (Issue 1/1995)

From Moscow, gay life under Communism plus new work from Alberto Manguel, Emma Donoghue, Lionel Blue, and Edmund White. Plus a country file on Turkey's bumpy road to democracy, with Yasar Kemal.

You're right. I cannot risk missing a single INDEX.

Send me the following issues:

❑	Issue 1-2/1994	£7
❑	Issue 3/1994	£7
❑	Issue 4-5/1994	£7
❑	Issue 6/1994	£7
❑	Issue 1/1995	£7
❑	**All five issues for only £30**	

Name ....

....

£_____ total. ❑ Cheque ❑ Visa ❑ MC ❑ American Express ❑ Diners' Club

Card no. ....

Expiry   Signature

Return to: **INDEX**, 33 Islington High Street, London N1 9LH
(UK orders can send to INDEX, Freepost, 33 Islington High Street, London N1 9BR.)

For faster service, fax your credit card order to 0171 278 1878.   A5C2

LETTER FROM MALAWI

JACK MAPANJE

GERRIT SERNE & PARTNER

Bitter-sweet tears

When I visited Malawi recently after three-and-a-half years of imprisonment followed by about four years in exile in the UK, I found myself doing what I had always desired but had not been allowed to do: floating in a boat at Cape Maclear, on Lake Malawi, with David Rubadiri, Malawi's most distinguished poet, well-known educationalist and critic, and Malawi's first representative to the United Nations 33 years ago. (He is rumoured to have been offered the same post by the new government and accepted.) Rubadiri's disagreement with Banda's repressive regime in the 1960s had forced him into such long exile that he was often mistaken for an East African, largely for his conspicuous contribution to the development of the East African literary scene. Rubadiri had returned home however, and together we were now drifting gently on the waves of Lake Malawi joking about the home we had missed these years, in the distant range of mountains across the blue waters of the lake. We were painfully aware however, that as in all dictatorships, the images of autocracy of the last 33 years would not be easy to dislodge from the various institutions and from people's minds; for example, that former President-for-Life Hastings Banda's intelligence apparatus was largely undiminished.

This notwithstanding, we were impressed by the people's determination to work even harder in order to succeed after Banda's absence from the political arena. The signs of free speech are everywhere. Some images of autocracy are inevitably crumbling, no longer occupying a prominent position in people's hearts, minds and the numerous liberal newspapers (whose number is gradually dwindling after the initial ebullience of the 1992 referendum and the 1994 general elections). The drinking places, the markets and the bus and railway stations often abruptly crack with loud laughter about how truly unfettered Malawi is without Banda. Stories of corruption even amongst the new politicians are frequent, largely because the new free press now reports them. Some of the laughter and criticism of authority borders on irresponsibility but it is honest and genuine. We have not seen anything like it in the last 33 years. Even the tourists have begun basking in the sun on the beaches of Lake Malawi without the endemic arbiters of the past years. Everyone is wishing the new Malawi well, albeit with some uneasiness, particularly after taking cognisance of the economic, health, educational and other problems that lie ahead for the new government to resolve.

And in spite of financial, philosophical or ideological constraints, the government is trying hard to rectify Banda's failures. The rural and urban communities are replete with committees intended to resolve something or other that Banda ignored.

There are committees for poverty alleviation; committees on information about AIDS and its avoidance; committees for free and compulsory primary education; committees for accountable disbursement of fertilisers and food-aid in the incessant drought; committees on easy communication, exchange and transportation of ideas and commodities between urban and rural areas. These and many more are mushrooming everywhere. I even overheard earnest government officials' intentions to educate and democratise such autocratic institutions as Banda's police force! Projects for the protection of the new constitution and civil liberties and for the improvement of ordinary people's lives, particularly

Mbumba, Malawi: the last round up

in the rural areas, no longer die in people's drawers or people's minds as of old. 'If only the rains came and we had the money, we would be a great nation; the true warm heart of Africa!' was one patriotic cry.

Meanwhile, Banda's economic outfit, reflected in the monopoly Press Holdings Conglomerate, is untainted by the new democratic culture. The joke in the drinking places is that there are two governments in Malawi today: Bakili Muluzi's political (democratically elected) government and Banda-Tembo's (despotic) economic government. Everybody knows who controls what. Everybody fears who will eventually predominate when the rains do not come and the chips are down. The matter is compounded by other global exigencies. Where talk of 'nationalisation' today triggers off unacceptable antediluvian socialist memories, nobody dares suggest that Muluzi's democratic government needs to contest the Banda-Tembo's monopoly economic empire for the country to elbow forward economically.

Today, I still recall the exciting meeting I had with friends and colleagues in the University of Malawi. 'I can even give a lecture on "Nudity and Art" without looking over my shoulder', says Malawi's best-known sculptor and artist, Berlings Kaunda. I still watch the canoes and nets of Cape Maclear fishermen coming home, drenched in Malawi's golden dusk. Rubadiri still gathers Cape Maclear beach children around him. They are crowded around a dugout canoe facing the island towards the vast blue waters of the bay. The clear, fresh and sober breakers are lap-lapping at our feet. He is enthralled by the story of a 12-year-old who went to the little village's free and compulsory primary school for the first time ever. Rubadiri's tears roll down his cheeks. I start whistling a childhood tune.

Today, from this distance, I must concede that I find it hard to comprehend the changes that have taken place in Malawi in such a short time. The rate at which events have transformed people's thinking and outlook is remarkable. I find myself still out of touch and still largely elated by Banda's sudden disappearance from the political landscape. But those playing the local politics in Malawi have gone beyond my distant ruminations. Their grave rumpus centres on four themes: the possibility of a witch-hunt developing as justice is sought through the courts for the actions of the Malawi Congress Party these 33 years; whether such a thing as genuine reconciliation with what one might call one's oppressors is possible and how this might be achieved; the wisdom of the government's recent change of the new constitution in order to introduce the post of second vice-president so that the country's three regions feel represented at the presidential level; and the corruption of the present politicians which is becoming a major subject of concern. Clearly, the Malawian situation is only a variant of other global instances of multi-party politics. South Africa immediately comes to mind. Doubtless comparisons ought to be made.

But nagging questions are being asked here. 'To what extent is the new government of national unity (without the Malawi Congress Party) going to be involved in punishing those who have committed crimes against humanity in the last three decades? Isn't this the government's ploy to divert energies from the real business of governing? How can we have genuine rapprochement with our oppressors when it is clear that what they want is to forget the atrocities they committed without atonement or without even admitting they were wrong? How long is the present coalition government of convenience going to last? How is the silver jubilee of Malawi's Writers' Group (which has contributed so much to the creation of the new democratic culture) to be celebrated next year?' Judging by the way these questions are being confronted, it is fair to assume that perhaps there will be no witch-hunt here; perhaps there will be bona fide reconstruction of the bridges broken these three decades. One thing is certain, nobody, not even the present Malawi Congress Party, seems to want the inequities of the last 33 years repeated.

The trouble with Malawi is that it is the whole nation, rather than the few in select urban or rural areas, that has lived under the culture of death, fear, lies and suspicion. Almost everyone, in villages as well as towns, has suffered at the hands of Banda. This includes Banda's own relatives. Banda's despotism appears to have excluded only Tembo's nephews and nieces and their relatives and friends. If further proof is required, enter any village in Malawi and ask the question: 'Who was forced to give up their property (eggs, goats, cows, money, businesses, etc); who was imprisoned, beaten up or beaten to death, thrown to crocodiles, exiled, *accidentalised* or other, in their extended family?' There will be many. Perhaps thousands. We all lived in fear of Banda and the various manifestations of his shadow, suspecting, imprisoning, killing one another on his behalf; often without the dictator's knowledge.

And the death of the four famous parliamentarians — the subject of the new government's first commission of inquiry, whose report, published in January 1995, unequivocally points the finger at Banda — was only one of many such incidents. I found people in Malawi speculating freely about the origin of other enigmatic deaths; the deaths of Dunduzu Chisiza, Lawrence Makata, Yatuta Chisiza, Masauko Chipembere and others in the 1960s and 1970s; the public hanging of Albert Muwalo, Silombera, Kanada; the assassination of Attati Mpakati in Zimbabwe and the bombing of Mkwapatira Mhango's entire family in Zambia and others in Mozambique. People began to cite instances of other inexplicable deaths they had not dared to talk about before, wherever Malawians had wandered. Those independent thinkers (usually called 'rebels' by informers or those under Banda's authority) who had been subjected to imprisonment, exile, death or other rare sanctions,

JACK MAPANJE

On His Excellency's house arrest

An excerpt

(Commiserations to International PEN Centre, Blantyre)

...

So, now that the febrile lion has accidentally fallen

Into the chasm of his own digging, let us resume
The true fight we abandoned thirty-three years ago
& begin to sing in the native tongues the old guards
Banned under the pretext of building our nation...
...

Yet today, after the lion has pulped his own cubs dead
Leaving the fragile village tainted in blood & after his
Chums across the valleys & beyond the seas have even
Shelved him; with lethal pythons & scorpions now tame;
Should we pour our libation on the steaming ancestral

Stones or shall we perhaps roll up our sleeve for other
More insular & baneful battles, when those old guards,
Not lionised enough by our euphoria, take their revenge?
Those grass huts Mbulaje's clients charred gobbling up
Whatever paracetamols they hacked their way still stand,

Watching his dreaming potholes that'll need our tender
& the human crocodiles their wicked amulets conceived
Or the endless cerebral malarias & the tuberculoses they
Loved to cast down dressed as AIDS. What chaos, what
Rare sneer won't they raise for our freedom to redress?

M'bulaje jwine, n'lyeje sadaka
M'bulaje jwine, n'lyeje sadaka
M'bulaje jwine, n'lyeje sadaka[1]

[1] *Kill another, for you to enjoy the funeral feast*

were now being publicly talked about and their heroism publicly acknowledged without apology in the new democratic culture. The political atmosphere is almost too healthy to be true; the economic chaos created by the previous government too worrying.

But too many Malawians have been exiled, imprisoned, detained, accidentalised, fed to crocodiles or have otherwise died without proper explanation for the new government to indulge in any meaningful witch-hunt. Giving Banda and his henchpersons (about a dozen altogether so far out of a population of 10 million) a malice-free trial is probably the one measure that would warrant authentic reconciliation between the past oppressors and those they oppressed.

The law must obviously take its course. Those who have suffered must feel somehow that their wrongs have been compensated for at three levels: legally — the culprits must be brought to the justice of proper courts (not Banda's traditional courts); financially — if there is money available it should be used to help the families of hundreds of illiterates living in the rural areas who have been wrongfully imprisoned; psychologically and spiritually — the oppressors should repent privately or publicly. Getting the oppressor to admit that he or she was wrong, without concomitant physical sanction might be enough recompense for some people who have been wronged. But the rule of law must take its course *without malice or vengeance*. The oppressor will need to feel that the victim has sincerely forgiven him or her. This will happen when justice is seen to be done *without malice*. The oppressed will need to feel compensated for the injustice inflicted on them. This will happen when some form of concession or atonement on the part of the oppressor is seen to be made. In other words, oppressors and oppressed must mutually feel genuinely reconciled.

Otherwise, everybody will continue indefinitely to justify their own stubborn actions. There cannot be enduring reparation when we do not feel adequately reconciled one to the other, however democratic the new culture. The debate on how best to arrest Banda's images of autocracy continues. It has just begun. As for the barbaric murder of the four parliamentarians, whatever is the final outcome, we hope that the new dispensation amply demonstrates that in future, political differences must never be resolved by the death of opposition or the elimination of opponents. Malawi threatens to be democratically provocative. We hope the ensuing thrills last without recourse to ugly personal vendettas. ❑

Death in the USA

'I believe the death penalty to be an effective means of protecting the public from cold-blooded killers who have no respect for innocent lives.

'I believe the death penalty is a just punishment and righteous retribution.

'Thanks to the death penalty, there isn't a chance in Hell that Ted Bundy or John Wayne Gacy will kill another innocent victim'

Gov William F Weld of Massachusetts

Testimony before the Joint Committee on Criminal Justice, H 4285, An Act Reinstituting the Death Penalty, Friday 1 July 1994

CAROLINE MOOREHEAD

Dead man walking

Until they were stopped not long ago, guards in San Quentin Penitentiary in California shouted 'dead man walking' whenever a man left his cell on death row. This haunting and poetic cry says much about the way Americans view those they plan to execute.

There is, however, nothing poetic in what is happening today on America's 38 death rows. Executions, stopped in 1972 after the US Supreme Court struck down most death penalty laws on grounds of unfairness, are once again on the increase. Two hundred and fifty-seven people have died — by lethal injection, electric chair, gas chamber, hanging or firing squad — since 1977; 2,870 are waiting on death row. As new crime bills carrying the death penalty are passed at federal level; as George Pataki, the new Republican governor of New York presses ahead with plans to reintroduce the death penalty, saying that he will auction Sing Sing's 'Old Sparkies', the electric chairs, for a quarter of a million dollars each and introduce lethal injections instead; and as Victim Support Groups grow more vocal in their calls for revenge and retribution, so many of these men and women can expect to die before too long. They may even do so in public, for a number of chat-show hosts have been applying to broadcast executions.

There have been protests throughout liberal America at the way in which death sentences are handed out disproportionately to minorities, the poor, the mentally ill and retarded, and those without adequate counsel. At least one black prisoner was executed in 1994 after being convicted by an all white jury, the prosecutor having struck all potential black jurors from the jury pool. Jury misinformation, misconduct and racial bias came to light just before a second man went to his death: these were not judged sufficient grounds for clemency. A third man, acknowledged to be seriously mentally ill, dropped his appeals and asked to be executed: the state complied. Shortly before retiring last year, Supreme Court Justice Harry A Blackmun declared that, in his opinion, the way the death penalty was now being administered was not just unconstitutional

Key:
L *Lethal injection*
G *Gas*
E *Electrocution*
H *Hanging*
F *Firing squad*

ENDEAVOR

COVER STORY

but 'fraught with arbitrariness, discrimination, caprice and mistake'. Sending a man who managed to produce belated evidence of innocence to his death on the grounds that the time had passed for a new appeal, he said, 'comes perilously close to simple murder'.

The USA is one of only four countries in the world — Pakistan, Yemen and Saudi Arabia are the others — that regularly sentence juveniles — those under the age of 18 when their crime was committed — to death. Though this practice has been outlawed as too barbaric elsewhere, it does not breach international agreements, for the US government took care to enter a reservation on this point before ratifying the relevant treaties. Nine juveniles have been executed in the last 10 years; there are 37 others on death row today.

One of those awaiting a lethal injection is Heath Wilkins. He was 16 when, together with four other runaway teenagers living rough in Avondal, Missouri, he killed a young mother of two small children during a liquor store hold up. His childhood had been grim: badly beaten by his mother, given marijuana when he was still in kindergarten, sent repeatedly to mental institutions, he had tried to commit suicide three times before the age of 10. Both defence and prosecution pronounced him too disturbed to stand trial, but he did; and after asking repeatedly for the death penalty, he got it. That was over nine years ago. He has

AMNESTY INTERNATIONAL

Nanjing, China 1983: posters announcing executions

been on death row in Missouri ever since, enduring the long process of appeals; on one occasion he was just 24 hours from execution. He now has two appeals left.

What makes the process so peculiar is that Wilkins, at 25, is no longer the disturbed teenager he was in 1985, but a young man desperate for a new and proper trial. Conscious of his terrible mistake in refusing all help and calling for his own death, he has to contemplate the likelihood that the other four teenagers who killed with him will be paroled, while he dies for the same crime.

Much of the rest of the world has not followed the execution-minded USA down this road. The long history of the abolition movement is usually said to have begun in Italy in 1764, when Cesare Beccaria published 'On Crimes and Punishments', a fierce attack on capital punishment. In 1786, taking Beccaria's treatise as a starting point, the Grand Duke Leopold of Tuscany drew up a new penal code, in which the death penalty was forbidden.

Venezuela, in 1863, became the first country to abolish it for all offences. Since World War II, and the Universal Declaration of Human Rights, which recognised each person's right to life, the campaign for abolition has been growing steadily, the Sixth Protocol to the European Convention on Human Rights being the first international agreement, when it came into force in 1985, to abolish the death penalty for all peace-time offences. Though 97 countries retain the death penalty, there are now 96 abolitionist countries — 54 having abolished it for all crimes, 15 for all but 'exceptional', ie wartime, crimes, and 27 de facto abolitionist, having had no execution for 10 years. Two countries on average are doing away with it every year, and with Turkey now de facto abolitionist, western Europe is today totally free of the death penalty. The eastern European states look likely to take the same path. One of the most encouraging of recent moves is a call by the parliamentary body of the 32-member Council of Europe for a treaty abolishing the death penalty for *all* crimes, without exception, even in wartime. States within the council currently retaining the death penalty would be obliged, under the new treaty, to set up commissions of enquiry, with a view to abolition.

Some hard cases, however, remain. China heads the league of countries with gruesome practices, and with well over 1,500 people executed every year, far exceeds all other places for numbers. The minimum legal age for criminal responsibility in China is seven, and 60 crimes, one of them hooliganism, carry the death penalty. These sentences are often handed out during rallies in stadiums, the convicts having been paraded through the streets in open trucks. Death, by firing squad, can follow within hours. There have recently been reports that China is trading in the kidneys and corneas taken from the bodies of executed prisoners, sometimes timing executions to fit in with medical requirements, and that prisoners are shot in the back or the head, depending on whether a cornea or a kidney is needed. Some are said to have their organs removed before execution. As the trade in body organs becomes more lucrative and medical progress makes transplants more successful, it may lead to an ever-increasing number of executions.

Far less numerous but just as shocking are the beheadings handed down under *sharia* law in Saudi Arabia for apostasy, certain acts of sabotage, treason or conspiracy against the state, some sexual offences and robbery with violence. Women are shot by firing squad, unless the crime is adultery — in which case they are stoned to death. Executions are carried out in major cities on a Friday, after midday prayers, usually in a square before the provincial governor's palace. There is no bar association in Saudi Arabia; a confession extracted under torture is sufficient for a conviction.

Public executions continue in Nigeria, where, on 2 August last year, 38 prisoners were shot by firing squad before a crowd of 20,000 people in Enugu, in the southeast. Most had been convicted by Robbery and Firearm Tribunals, where there is no right of appeal. One young man, 24 -year-old Simeon Agbo, rose to his feet an hour after the shooting, bleeding from his shoulders and his stomach, and begged for clemency. He was thrown, still alive, on to the truck carrying the 37 corpses and was never heard of again.

For some time now there have been complaints that holding a condemned prisoner indefinitely on death row amounts to the 'inhuman and degrading treatment' proscribed under international law. A test case in Jamaica has recently led to a new limit — five years — on the length of time a person may wait on death row. It has resulted in unsettling and not always satisfactory implications (see 'The quality of mercy' p163).

The appalling conditions on most death rows played their part in this debate. 'Combine a hospital ward for the terminally ill,' suggested William Schabao, professor of law at Quebec University in an article not long ago, 'an institution of the criminally insane, and an ultra-maximum security wing in a penitentiary, and one begins to approach the horror of death row.' Though few death rows, perhaps, have quite the horror of Japan's cells for the condemned, where men have spent decades, most of the time in solitary confinement, before execution. Sadamichi Hirasawa cheated the executioner last year by dying before reaching the gallows. He was 94, and had spent 37 years on death row. He had appealed 17 times for a retrial.

Since its foundation in 1961, Amnesty International has led the campaign against the death penalty, which it regards in fundamental breach of all human rights international treaties. One by one, its more brutal aspects are being eroded — at least in theory. The UN Human Rights Commission decision, not long ago, to ban death by gas chamber as 'inhuman treatment' has marked another step, even if it begs the question of how you ever kill a person 'humanely'. For Justice Harry Blackmun, passionate advocate of abolition after 20 years of constitutional analysis, these minute concessions constitute no more than 'tinkering with the machinery of death'. Yet this remains a subject more characterised by contradictions and questions than most. Why continue with the death penalty at all, when study after study fails to come up with convincing evidence that the death penalty deters people from murder, acts of terror or politically-motivated crimes? What is to be put in its place, if it is accepted that prolonged periods on death row are 'inhuman'? How do

Calabar, Nigeria 1985: executed for armed robbery

you justify hanging a man by his neck until dead, if hanging him by his arms in agony is universally outlawed as torture? 'Revenge' is an integral part of several legal systems, including the Islamic; how do you handle the increasing desire for revenge behind the widespread popular support for execution in countries like Britain today? In a world increasingly fearful of lawlessness and economic and political collapse, where the pressure to toughen up anti-crime measures grows rather than lessens, 'tinkering', depressing as it is, may for the moment be the manner in which the move towards total abolition is condemned to go. ❑

Further reading on the USA and the death penalty:

Amnesty International: Conditions for death row prisoners in H-Unit, Oklahoma State Penitentiary *(May 1994, 32pp, £1.50),* Open letter to the President on the death penalty *(January 1994, 21pp, £1.50);* Possible reinstatement of the death penalty in New York *(January 1995, 4pp, £1);* Follow up to Amnesty International's open letter to the President on the death penalty *(January 1995, 5pp, £1.00);* Developments on the death penalty during 1994 *(January 1995, 22pp, £1.50)*

Death Penalty Information Center: Richard C Dieter On the front line: law enforcement views on the death penalty *(February 1995, 25pp)*

Information overleaf *compiled with help from Amnesty, the UN and the Centre for Capital Punishment studies, University of Westminster, London* ❑

ROBERT MAHARAJH

The ultimate penalty

Since the last UN survey in 1988 the total number of 'retentionist' countries has decreased from 101 to 97. Turkey has now passed the ten-year limit, leaving western Europe entirely abolitionist.

In eastern Europe the trend is less clear: countries which abolished in a mood of post-Communist optimism now find themselves with an alarming crime rate and renewed calls for the ultimate deterrent.

Almost all the states of the Middle East retain the penalty under Islamic law; most of the Caribbean states do so through popular demand. In the US the current climate of fear makes pro-penalty rhetoric a definite vote-winner, as even Democrats have recognised.

South and Central America continue to follow the trend towards abolition, but the region's history shows that reversals occur at times of political instability.

In sub-Saharan Africa six countries have abolished since 1988, but there is still strong support for the penalty. Furthermore, as in South America, 'unofficial' killings are widespread and so the figures given can be misleading.

The Asia/Pacific region shows encouraging signs, with Cambodia and Hong Kong now completely abolitionist. Nevertheless, the main offenders in this region — Japan, Pakistan and China — are among the worst in the world, and show no signs of changing policy. ❑

KEY

R *Retentionist (ie countries which retain and use the death penalty for ordinary crimes)*

AC *Abolitionist for all crimes (ie countries whose laws do not provide for the death penalty for any crime)*

OC *Abolitionist for ordinary crimes only (ie countries whose laws provide for the death penalty only for exceptional crimes such as crimes under military law or crimes committed in exceptional circumstances such as wartime)*

DF *Abolitionist de facto (ie countries which retain the death penalty for ordinary crimes but have not executed anyone during the past 10 years, with date of last execution);*

** *no executions since independence*

Africa (sub-Saharan)

Angola	AC
Benin	R
Botswana	R
Burkina Faso	R
Burundi	DF:1982
Cameroon	R
Cape Verde	AC
Central African Republic	DF:1981
Chad	R
Chile	R
Congo	DF:1982
Comoros	DF:**
Cote d'Ivoire	DF
Djibouti	DF:**
Equatorial Guinea	R
Eritrea	R
Ethiopia	R
Gabon	R
Gambia	AC
Ghana	R
Guinea	R
Guinea-Bissau	AC
Kenya	R
Lesotho	R
Liberia	R
Madagascar	DF:1958
Malawi	R
Mauritania	R
Mauritius	R
Mozambique	AC
Namibia	AC
Niger	DF:1976
Nigeria	R
Rwanda	DF:1982
Sao Tome & Principe	AC
Senegal	DF:1967
Seychelles	OC
Sierra Leone	R
Somalia	R
South Africa	R
Suriname	DF:1984
Swaziland	R
Togo	DF
Tanzania	R
Uganda	R
Zaire	R
Zambia	R
Zimbabwe	R

Asia & the Pacific

Afghanistan	R
Australia	AC
Azerbaijan	R
Bangladesh	R
Bhutan	DF:1964
Brunei	DF:1957
Cambodia	AC
China	R
Fiji	OC
Hong Kong	AC
India	R
Indonesia	R
Japan	R
Kazakhstan	R
Kiribati	AC
Kyrgyzstan	R
Laos	R

Malaysia	R
Maldives	DF:1952
Mali	DF:1980
Marshall Islands	AC
Micronesia	AC
Mongolia	R
Myanmar	R
Nauru	DF:**
Nepal	OC
New Zealand	AC
North Korea	R
Pakistan	R
Papua New Guinea	DF:1950
Philippines	DF:1976
Samoa, Western	DF:**
Singapore	R
Solomon Islands	AC
South Korea	R
Sri Lanka	DF:1976
Tajikistan	R
Taiwan	R
Thailand	R
Tonga	DF:1982
Turkmenistan	R
Tuvalu	AC
Uzbekistan	R
Vanuatu	AC
Vietnam	R

Caribbean

Antigua & Barbuda	R
Bahamas	R
Barbados	R
Bermuda	DF:1977
Cuba	R
Dominica	R
Dominican Republic	AC
Grenada	R
Guyana	R
Haiti	AC
Jamaica	R
St Christopher & Nevis	R
St Lucia	R
St Vincent & the Grenadines	R
Trinidad & Tobago	R

Eastern Europe

Albania	R
Armenia	R
Belarus	R
Bosnia-Hercegovina	R
Bulgaria	R
Croatia	AC
Czech Republic	AC
Estonia	R
Georgia	R
Hungary	AC
Latvia	R
Lithuania	R
Macedonia	AC
Moldova	R
Poland	R
Romania	AC
Russia	R
Slovakia	AC
Slovenia	AC
Ukraine	R
Yugoslavia, Federal Republic	R

Western Europe

Andorra	AC
Austria	AC
Belgium	DF:1950
Cyprus	OC
Denmark	AC
Finland	AC
France	AC
Germany	AC
Greece	AC
Iceland	AC
Ireland	AC
Italy	AC
Liechtenstein	AC
Luxembourg	AC
Malta	OC
Monaco	AC
Netherlands	AC
Norway	AC
Portugal	AC
San Marino	AC
Spain	OC
Sweden	AC
Switzerland	AC
Turkey	DF:1984
United Kingdom	OC
Vatican City	AC

Middle East & North Africa

Algeria	R
Bahrain	DF:1977
Egypt	R
Iran	R
Iraq	R
Israel	OC
Jordan	R
Lebanon	R
Libya	R
Morocco	R
Oman	R
Qatar	R
Saudi Arabia	R
Sudan	R
Syria	R
Tunisia	R
United Arab Emirates	R
Yemen	R

North America

Canada	OC
United States of America	R
Mexico	OC

South & Central America

Argentina	OC
Belize	R
Bolivia	DF:1974
Brazil	OC
Colombia	AC
Costa Rica	AC
Ecuador	AC
El Salvador	OC
Guatemala	R
Honduras	AC
Nicaragua	AC
Paraguay	OC
Panama	AC
Peru	OC
Uruguay	AC
Venezuela	AC

CHRISTOPHER HITCHENS

Why Americans like the penalty of death

The American culture contains at least one enormous and self-evident contradiction, and American politics and institutions reflect this contradiction in very bizarre ways. The contradiction is more easily quoted than stated, because it is not a contradiction of which its exemplars are very perfectly aware. Coming right down to it then, the very person who sits next to you on that United Airlines long haul, and who sings high about how 'this is the greatest country God made' and 'the freest society on God's earth' and (lapsing into secular patriotic vernacular) 'the land of the free and the home of the brave', will most likely warn you, a few free drinks and a few mileage-club miles later, that it is nowhere safe to walk the streets, that old people are afraid to leave their homes, that children are in constant peril of every kind of sordid molestation and that only ruin and bankruptcy await the bold entrepreneur.

Forcing one to notice the same paradox in a different way, the more ideological types will say that state power needs to be rolled back, and that 'big government' is the enemy of the American ideal, and add that it's high time that the Supreme Court mandated the death penalty. I know a number of honest libertarians who refuse on principle to grant the state the right of life and death over the citizen, but even they make this point as if admitting that there is an 'irony' involved: in other words, that rugged American individualists generally demand that the state be more interventionist on this front. The point was nicely caught by a recent note in the *New York Times*, following the defeat of Mario Cuomo as New York's governor: 'Eleven days after he took office, George Pataki, New York's pro-death penalty governor, sent Thomas Grasso, a pro-death

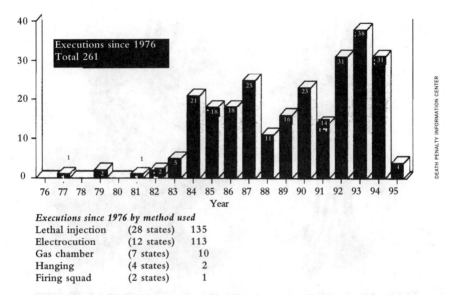

Executions since 1976
Total 261

DEATH PENALTY INFORMATION CENTER

Year

Executions since 1976 by method used

Lethal injection	(28 states)	135
Electrocution	(12 states)	113
Gas chamber	(7 states)	10
Hanging	(4 states)	2
Firing squad	(2 states)	1

*Some states authorise more than one method

penalty murderer, back to Oklahoma to await death by lethal injection.'

In America, capital punishment is *so* popular that even the denizens of death row support it! Mr Grasso had indeed demanded to be returned to a death penalty state for execution, and not long ago a child-slayer described in court as a 'calcified sadist' begged to be despatched by the notoriously auto-erotic means of strangulation. His wishes, too, were met, even though meeting them involved a change in the state laws governing execution. Not even this pornographic satire on the law was enough to stir any queasy afterthoughts. Populism rules and what populism wants, populism gets.

With the exception of Japan, no other advanced industrial country executes people any more, but then no other 'advanced industrial country' is so close to the memory of frontier justice. No other similar society is so riven by ethnic and social rivalry. No other comparable nation has such a lurid gun-club following, or such an intimate acquaintance with domestic and civil homicide. So, at least the arguments run, often from both supporters and opponents. Yet in the past generations, Europe has been far more soaked in violence and revenge-killings, and the frontier ethic is not unknown in Ireland or Greece or Italy or Spain. Many other

yOU..

..TAKE AN EYE FOR AN EYE ..THEN.. JUSTICE <u>IS</u> BLIND

PHILIP WILSON

countries have horrid and intractable tribal quarrels, or civil-war memories. As for the violent crime business, it is true that America lives a crime drama on its screens and in its fiction and fantasy, and has exported the genre worldwide, but it is even more a fact that violent crime is falling by every useful measurement. (In New York, homicide rates have halved in the tenure of the present attorney general.) This is for the simple and intelligible reason that violent crime correlates raggedly, if at all, with other variables such as race, poverty, immigration or social dislocation such as unemployment. It does, however, correlate very closely with testosterone levels; in other words, with the delinquency of young men in packs. And in America, the average age is rising, so that violent crimes per head are in decline.

This, perhaps, is to be too calculating. The violent crimes that do occur and are reported, are often of a peculiar heinousness that would exhaust the outrage deserved by many more crimes committed in more banal ways. In a very rich, secure and highly-policed country, millions of citizens just do not *feel* safe. And their fear must be assuaged. It is not easily assuaged by a Constitution that appears to safeguard the rights of the defendant, that allows horse-and-cart loopholes to clever defence lawyers, and which prohibits 'cruel and unusual punishment' — the only form of words under which the penalty of death has so far been legally contestable in the Supreme Court.

There is, however, a small but significant group of Americans that remains, or has become, convinced that the death penalty is a moral and legal failure. This group is drawn from the ranks of those who have to administer it. The former chief executioner at San Quentin prison, who was personally responsible for the largest number of despatchings in American history, wrote that it had had no discernible or measurable influence on the murder rate, and that it was in any case 'a privilege of the poor'. In a recent interview with David von Drehle of the *Washington Post*, Ray Marky of the Florida attorney general's office said the following: 'If we had deliberately set out to create a chaotic system, we couldn't have come up with anything worse. It's a merry-go-round; it's ridiculous; it's so clogged-up only an arbitrary few ever get it. I don't get any damn pleasure out of the death penalty and I never have. And frankly, if they abolished it tomorrow, I'd go get drunk in celebration.'

Ray Marky's testimony is significant because Florida has been the pace-setting state in executing convicts ever since the Supreme Court threw the issue back to state governments in the early 1970s. Governor Bob Martinez signed 139 death warrants in four years (sometimes, like Governor Bill Clinton of Arkansas, timing clusters of executions for tightly-contested electoral dramas). 'Old Sparky', as Florida's electric chair is obscenely or as some like to phrase it 'affectionately' known, has been in regular and continuous employment. But Florida's reputation for violent crime remains no less deserved and, perhaps equally important, the feeding of death row prisoners to 'Old Sparky' appears to be determined by some kind of lottery. Thomas Knight, for example, has been on death row in Florida for *20 years*. It took 10 years to incinerate the fabled serial killer Ted Bundy. Other prisoners, many of whom have committed crimes much less atrocious, are executed with relative speed. Nobody will be startled to hear that these have a tendency to be poor, to be non-white, and to be under-represented by counsel.

It is the latter point which has 'got to' Ray Marky. In an average case, if a defendant *can* get hold of a lawyer, the chances of getting a stay of execution, a judicial review of the sentence or even a fresh trial are so high that all possibility of consistency in the application of the supreme penalty has been lost. This would be true even if it were a penalty imposed at the federal level. But the mishmash of conflicting statutes operating state by state (such that Governor Pataki has literally to 'extradite' a man who says he wishes to be hanged in Oklahoma) makes an already anomalous situation into an anomaly in itself.

'People think of capital punishment as something that is applied to "the other,"' says Leslie Abramson. Now celebrated as the stunning reversal-of-fortune attorney in the case of the Menendez brothers, she began her career as California's most intransigent opponent of the gas chamber, and has saved countless defendants from the death penalty. 'They never think of it as something that could happen to one of their own.' Insofar as this can be tested as a 'perception', it holds up quite well. Black voters, who are generally very tough on law and order questions, always evince revulsion against capital punishment when polled as a group. This is what is vulgarly called a 'race memory' — the gibbet and the chair as the ultimate sanction of racism and exploitation. Black Americans also form the majority of those (at least two dozen in this century, according to a survey by the *Stanford Law Review*) who were executed while guiltless of any crime.

But though it's obvious that the death penalty is historically connected to racism, it may be reductionist to explain its popular appeal purely in this fashion. There are many countries and societies where crude opinion considers the crime question to be a subset of the gypsy question, the immigrant question, the religious question and so forth, but where democratic politicians are not under overwhelming pressure to sanction a penalty that they know to be ineffective and barbarous. It may make more sense to see the high vote for the death penalty as a version of the longing for simplicity.

In a very large and diverse and geographically-extended society like the American, where widely separated communities are knit together largely by information, a crisp and certain 'message' of any kind is relatively rare. Congressional proceedings are very muddy and extremely protracted; international relations highly complex and arcane; the pace of news and salesmanship often bewildering; the school system a mystery to many parents. Encounters with the bureaucracy are thwarting and frustrating. Might it not be salutary — might it not be *nice* — to see a grisly malefactor, just for once, taken straight from the dock and put up against a wall? Might it not be *clarifying,* and a good example for the rising generation? I confess to having thought this a few times myself (especially at the time of the Watergate hearings and the Oliver North trial) and to have felt cheated by the blizzard of paperwork and obfuscation and 'the law's delay'. The thirst for justice in America is kept permanently unslaked by a corrupt legal system to which only the rich have real access, so populist resentment is not to be wondered at. One healthy consequence, if one may speak ironically, is that nobody ever bothers to put forward the old and discredited argument about capital punishment as a 'deterrent'. People are honest enough to state that they only desire it as a release; as a cathartic action of moral abhorrence and irreparable retribution. Well, at least that clears *that* up — though of course it's odd in a society which contains such an apparent plurality of believing Christians. (Confessing the failure of capital punishment as a legal weapon, New York's attorney general Robert Morgenthau wrote recently that the Lord had said 'vengeance is mine.' He probably had tactical reasons to confine himself to the Old Testament, though even that manages to contain the First Commandment.)

Yet the United States, which is constitutionally prohibited from establishing any state-sponsored religion, still has a civil one. And that civil religion is law. Lawyers are the moral and the fictional protagonists of society, supplying everything from the bestsellers to the TV series to the movies as well as the real-life confrontations. And it is the cunning and complexity of the law that robs public opinion of its

Vengeance is Mine

PHILIP WILSON

prey. At least since the belated statute against lynching took effect in the early years of this century, local worthies have been cheated of the right to immediate justice. Even the most appalling felon, equipped with no more than a bored and court-appointed attorney, can play out his frayed string for a year or two, while his victims (or their surviving relatives) bite their knuckles.

A very sinister change is involved, then, in recent attempts to change the law governing execution. According to a decision of the new Clarence Thomas-type Supreme Court, a defendant on death row who has exculpatory evidence can still be put to death if he fails to present that evidence past a certain deadline. So the much-loved Hollywood trope, of the last-minute telegram from the governor to the prison, is also for the chop. (I once waited for an execution at the notorious Parchman Prison Farm in Mississippi, where, as it happens, the black man who was gassed was later proven innocent, but where even as he waited for death it was evident to the warders that he had not had a fair trial or a decent lawyer. At Parchman, gassings were always scheduled for five minutes past the hour, because Chief Justice Earl Warren had once telephoned with a reprieve right on deadline and been told he was a few seconds too late.)

The new majority in Congress also wants to shorten the appeals process as being too bureaucratic and too much subject to procrastination and lawyerly manoeuvring. With this change, I think, the popularity of capital punishment will face a much more serious test than it has faced for generations. Until now, it has derived its support in much the same way as other supposed 'deterrents' — namely, by being unused. As it spreads, with Supreme Court and congressional complicity, across the states, its installation is certain to prove a disappointment. And what is more, it will more and more manifest its contradictions. A vile murderer will cop a plea here; an incompetent one-time killer will get the chair there. Innocent people will infallibly be shot or given lethal injections. The cost of the death row system, which is much more than some people imagine, will become more apparent. Above all, and even with 'speeded-up' terminations (because the speeded-up ones will certainly be the ones that give trouble when investigated), there will be a cultural conflict between America's exaggerated respect for 'due process' and America's political need for a 'tough on crime' totem. Like Mr Pataki's cynical prisoner Mr Grasso, populists may learn to beware of what they demand, because they may just get it. ❑

ARYEH NEIER

A special cruelty

There is a random and arbitrary quality about the death penalty. Often it is used more as a political convenience than a measure of justice

Since George Pataki was elected as governor of New York State last November, everyone has known that capital punishment would again become the law in New York.

The legislation now nearing adoption would apply to an estimated 15 to 20 per cent of the 2,300 murders committed each year in New York State. A larger number would be covered except that an effort has been made by the new governor's aides to draft the law in a way that complies with US Supreme Court decisions upholding the constitutionality of certain capital punishment laws.

Despite the legislation, unless there is an as yet unimaginable increase in the extent and intensity of the public sentiment responsible for the re-enactment of the death penalty, no one anticipates that 400 or 500 persons each year will actually be executed in New York. If the experience of other states that have restored the death penalty is repeated in New York, the number actually executed will be closer to four or five a year than to 400 or 500.

Though it may seem odd, it is the fact that the law will actually be carried out so infrequently (and, therefore, so arbitrarily and capriciously) that is at the heart of my own opposition to the death penalty. There is a special cruelty in carrying out executions of just a small handful of those to whom the law actually applies. Inevitably, in such circumstances, the factors that determine who is chosen for execution include matters that are unrelated to the actual crimes they committed.

An illustrative case is that of John Spenkelink, the first man executed in Florida after that state restored the death penalty nearly two decades ago, and the first man executed against his will anywhere in the USA after a decade-long de facto moratorium on executions. (One man, Gary Gilmore, had been executed by firing squad in Utah two years earlier

CAMERA PRESS

GARY GILMORE

The land lord

Feeling a beckoning wind blow thru
The chambers of my soul I knew
It was time entered in
I climbed within and stared about —
I was home indeed my very seed
A mirror of me reflecting myself
From every curve and line and shelf
Every surface there Every texture bare
Every color tone and value Each sound
Pride Hate Vanity
Sloth Waste Insanity Lust Envy Want
Ignorance black and green
I felt myself at every turning
Set my very mind to burning
Face to face no way to dodge
Headlong I tumbled thru this lodge
I felt and met alone myself
A red scream rushed forth But I caught
it back and checked its force
It crescendoed into a hopeless heavy weight
in the blood and fell...
A beat of wing I felt and heard
Not at all like any bird
Overhead I saw myself contorted black
and brown and twisted mean — borne aloft
by a gray bat wing — growing from
my shoulders there...
One thing was peculiar clear
There was no scorn to menace here
This is just the way it is
Laid bare to the bone
And I built this house I alone
I am the Land Lord here

Gary Gilmore was executed by firing squad at Utah State prison in 1977

© Out of the Night: Writings from Death Row, *compiled and edited by Marie Mulvy Roberts (New Clarion Press, 1994)* after opposing efforts by lawyers to block his execution.) By every reasonable criterion, his death sentence should have been commuted. A drifter, Spenkelink had killed a fellow drifter, an older, larger and stronger man who had forcibly sodomised him. A Florida jury did not believe Spenkelink's claim that he had killed in self-defence; he had waited until the man who raped him was asleep, the jury determined, and therefore was guilty of premeditated murder.

As murders go, this was not one calculated to arouse particular outrage. Yet the governor of Florida and his Cabinet, who had the power to commute Spenkelink's death sentence, did not do so. Spenkelink was white, and the next several persons in line for execution were black. When restoration of the death penalty had been debated in Florida, opponents had argued that it would be applied in a racially discriminatory way. Commuting the sentence of a white killer and executing the blacks who were in line after him would have ensured the renewal and intensification of such charges. Accordingly, John Spenkelink was electrocuted in May 1979 so that the state of Florida could prove that it was an equal opportunity executioner.

Thirty years ago, as executive director of the New York Civil Liberties Union, I took part in the legislative lobbying that led to the repeal of capital punishment in New York. The same year, the Iowa, Vermont and West Virginia legislatures also abolished the death penalty and, the previous autumn, it had been ended by popular referendum in Oregon where the abolitionist side won 60 per cent of the vote. Though there has been a sea change in public opinion since those heady days when we seemed to be making progress for civil rights on every front, and though polls suggest that an overwhelming majority of Americans now favour the death penalty, there is little conviction behind today's popular demand for capital punishment. Hardly anyone imagines that executions will actually affect the crime rate. Pro-death penalty politicians get elected, and new death laws get enacted for symbolic reason; capital punishment is one of those issues that establishes on which side of a cultural divide Americans stand. It establishes their determination to be tough on crime, even if it has no effect on criminality. On those grounds, New York will now join most other states in putting to death a few persons each year who are chosen to pay this penalty because, as happened to John Spenkelink, circumstances make it more convenient to execute them than to spare them. ❏

HUGO BEDAU

PHILIP WILSON

Dangerous liaisons

Capital punishment is a vote winner. Democrats are joining Republicans in pressing home the advantage

The year is 2020. As we look across the USA with an eye on the death penalty, what do we see? Executions now occur two or three times a week somewhere in the nation. Despite speed-up procedures, processing appeals in capital cases now occupies half to two-thirds of the time and energies of all the appellate courts, state and federal. Fewer and fewer of these appeals result in benefits for the defendant as appellate courts routinely deny the petitions. Nevertheless, the pile-up on death rows continues at an ever growing pace thanks to the increase in the variety of capital crimes and the eagerness of trial juries to bring in death sentences. Ten thousand convicts, mostly men and mostly killers of whites, now await final disposition of their death sentences. Every state has had to build special prisons just for its death row convicts. The extra security costs continue to mount each year, but the general public would rather spend US$1,000 on punishment than US$100 on prevention. Within the past decade all the state jurisdictions that had long abolished the death penalty, including Michigan, with no executions since 1846, have restored the death penalty, without any evidence that their citizens now receive greater protection than before. No-one remembers the last time a governor granted executive clemency to a death row convict.

All politicians in whatever office, from mayor or district attorney to senator, governor, or president profess unswerving commitment to the death penalty. Some years ago, the national Democrat Party joined the Republicans in endorsing capital punishment in their party platforms. Since the defeat of Governor Mario Cuomo in New York in 1994, no eloquent public voice has been heard objecting to the death penalty. Thanks to litigation by some death row inmates, supported by television stations and the American Civil Liberties Union, executions are now regularly shown during the morning news. With the failure of frequent executions to show any reduction in the crime rate and also public frustration over the seemingly painless and squeaky clean effects of death by lethal injection, some politicians agitate for a return to more gruesome methods of execution reflecting public discontent.

Survey research year after year reports a large and stable majority, about 80-85 per cent of the adult population regardless of age, gender, race, political party or socio-economic class, in favour of executions. Recent academic research confirms the results of earlier investigations in showing no discernible benefits from the death penalty.

Public opposition to the death penalty has virtually ceased in any organised form. The National Coalition to Abolish the Death Penalty, organised in 1976, dissolved when its then executive director and board of directors announced that their efforts would be better rewarded if as individuals they devoted their time and money to entirely different issues with more prospect of success. In recent years, Amnesty International, the American Civil Liberties Union, the NAACP Legal Defense Fund — the three stalwart founding members of the National Coalition — have literally dropped all efforts to implement their long-standing policies against the death penalty.

In short, the death penalty in the US is entrenched more strongly today than at any time in the nation's history.

What I have presented is a not unreasonable prophecy, given prevailing trends in the USA today. Thirty or 35 years ago there was no such thing as the political significance or political relevance of the death penalty. No candidates ran for national or local office on a platform endorsing or seeking to restore the death penalty; no political party took any interest in the subject. Young, old, black, white, male, female, educated or not, people were generally uninterested, and those who did take an interest, particularly those who opposed it, cut across all demographic variables. That is not true today.

Public opinion in the United States is constant at around 80 per cent of the public for the death penalty; a very small percentage, maybe 15 per cent, against it; and an even smaller percentage undecided. Results depend on who is doing the survey and the scope of the questions. If the public is asked: 'Would you favour the death penalty if there were an alternative punishment of life without parole?' support for the death penalty drops radically by around half.

But support for the penalty runs deep. In state after state, year after year and to an increasing degree, bills are filed to augment, increase, speed up and in other ways make the death penalty laws at the state level more effective. In Tennessee, for instance, which already has the death penalty, a bill was filed during 1994 to allow the death penalty to be implemented not only for first degree murder but also for solicitation to commit first degree murder. While the US has held that the mandatory death sentence for first degree murder is unconstitutional, another bill was filed to amend the Tennessee constitution to require the death sentence for all convictions for first degree murder. Another bill would bar post-conviction appeals from those convicted of first degree murder and sentenced to death if filed more than five years after the initial review. Very often evidence of the incompetence of the attorney at trial or exculpatory evidence tending to establish the innocence of the convicted offender isn't known or available to bring to court within five years after the trial.

Today, New York does not have the death penalty, but with the defeat of Governor Mario Cuomo by his opponent, the Republican Party candidate who ran essentially on two issues, lowering taxes and restoring the death penalty, it's virtually certain that in less than a year it will. Here, too, there is a range of bills that would extend its use and make it mandatory for murder.

If the politicians in New York and Tennessee put the issue to the public in those states, these bills would pass. Given the mood of the state legislatures, however, there is no need to turn to public referenda. In New York, as of March 1995, Governor George Pataki is on the verge of getting a bill enacted that would return the death penalty for some types of murder (not, however, a mandatory death penalty, because that would be flagrantly unconstitutional).

Even the constitution is infected with the status of public opinion on this issue. In 1972 Justice Brennan, writing in opposition to the death penalty and arguing its necessary incompatibility with the federal constitution, said that one of the factors that could show that it was a cruel and unusual punishment was that it was a severe punishment infrequently applied because people don't want it applied.

It has now become virtual political suicide, or is believed to be virtual political suicide for an incumbent governor to carry out any serious executive review in capital cases where the outcome might be a commutation of sentence. Commutation of death sentences in the USA 20, 30 or 40 years ago was not uncommon. It was a rare governor in death penalty states in those days who never commuted a death sentence.

The best reason of all for commuting a death sentence is the discovery of evidence subsequent to the court proceedings proving innocence. Such considerations played an important role in bringing about executive clemency in capital cases earlier this century. Rarely do they do so today.

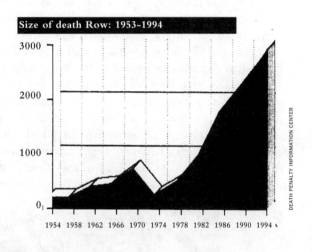

Size of death Row: 1953-1994

DEATH PENALTY INFORMATION CENTER

The presidential election of 1988 demonstrated the politicisation of the death penalty by its use as a device to win votes for Vice-President George Bush and to target his opponent, Governor Michael Dukakis, as unsympathetic to the plight of the average American.

In the 1992 election, the death penalty played rather a different role but was even more prominent. In the spring of that year, the Democrats had to choose their candidate to run against President George Bush, whose position for the death penalty was well established. Of the five candidates, Governor Bill Clinton from Arkansas made it perfectly clear, in contrast to his opponents, that he was the only one who had actually presided over an execution. And he did it again. He interrupted his campaign in New Hampshire to return to Arkansas, to be present while a very controversial death penalty case went to its conclusion. Clinton did not intervene; it would have meant the end of his candidacy. Such a situation would have been unimaginable in 1952, or 1962.

But 1992 was nothing compared to legislative elections of 1994. In October of that year, columnist Ellen Goodman wrote in the *Boston Globe*: 'Today each candidate is self-cast as a crime fighter, as if the Senate or the governor's mansion were a police station. Opponents crop up in ads like defendants in a line-up in the grainy black and white film once reserved for Willie Horton. The ads have come to imitate the crime news they interrupt. A rape victim stars in one spot, the mother of an assault victim stars in another. In Texas one of the Bush brothers, George Jr, ran an ad showing a man abducting a woman in a parking lot. Never mind that the abductor was the sound man and the abductee the make-up woman for the commercial. To prove their credibility in saying "I understand", candidates tell their personal stories on the airwaves... To further prove their toughness on crime, most candidates are topping each other in calls for longer, swifter, surer punishment... An inseparable part of these political scare tactics is that there is so little connection between fear and punishment, between public anxieties and the political solutions. The crime debate, says the dean of the Northeastern University School of Criminal Justice, is enough to make a criminologist sick. As for the

PHILIP WILSON

death penalty, he says, it doesn't accomplish much, except to get people elected.'

Item from an editorial in the *New York Times* of October: 'Families of murder victims have heartbreaking stories to tell. Candidates for political office all over the country are displaying the distasteful tendency to exploit these stories for their own benefit. This is a shameful new form of victim abuse, a shame compounded in the politicians' fraudulent use of families' bereavement to argue for the death penalty and to depict an opponent as soft on crime...'

The picture that emerges of this most recent election in the USA is that just about everybody running for elective office, from dog catcher to district attorney, from senator to governor, from congresswoman to justice of the courts, sees crime as the issue and the death penalty as the solution — if we can believe the politicians.

There are other symptoms that show the combination of public support for the death penalty and its politicisation. One: the way in which members of the family of the victim are playing an increasingly visible role at executions and on television, urging the execution of the murderer of their loved one.

Two: the growing interest in putting executions on television, live with the eight o'clock news on morning television. That has yet to happen, but the curious combination of civil libertarians who believe the broadcast media should have every access to events that the print media do and some death row convicts who would like to have their executions televised, may someday prevail. It is the agitation rather than the actual event that is significant. Three: the consequence of the activity of the Supreme Court. Since the mid-1970s, the Supreme Court has said that during the sentencing phase of a capital trial, the defendant is entitled to have any evidence brought forward by his counsel and put before the jury that might mitigate his crime and incline the jury favourably toward a sentence other than death. Over the years some, particularly prosecuting attorneys, have protested at the inequity of such a situation. As a result, surviving members of the victim's family, friends, employers or whoever, are now free to give testimony that will assist the prosecution in securing the death sentence. The argument in favour of this development has been

Continued on page 116

MUMIA ABU-JAMAL

A bright, shining hell

Imagine.

Imagine living, eating, sleeping, relieving oneself, daydreaming, weeping — but mostly waiting — in a room about the size of your bathroom.

Now imagine doing all those things — but mostly waiting — for the rest of your life.

Imagine waiting — waiting — waiting — to die.

I don't have to imagine.

I 'live' in one of those rooms, like about 3,000 other men and women in 37 states across the United States.

It's called 'Death Row'.

I call it 'Hell'.

Welcome to Hell.

Each of the states that have death rows has a different system for its 'execution cases' varying from the relatively open to the severely restrictive.

Some states, like California and Texas, allow their 'execution cases' work, education and/or religious service opportunities, for out-of-cell-time up to eight hours daily.

Pennsylvania locks its 'execution cases' down 23 hours a day, five days a week; 24 hours the other two days.

At the risk of quoting Mephistopheles, I repeat:

Welcome to Hell.

A hell erected and maintained by human governments and blessed by black-robed judges.

A hell that allows you to see your loved ones, but not to touch them.

A hell situated in America's rural boondocks, hundreds of miles away from most families.

A white, rural hell, where most of the caged captives are black and urban.

It is an American way of death.

Contrary to what one might suppose, this hell is the easiest one to enter in a generally hellish criminal justice system. Why? Because, unlike any other case, those deemed potential capital cases are severely restricted during the jury selection phase, as any juror who admits opposition to the death penalty is immediately removed, leaving only those who are fervent death penalty supporters in the pool of eligible jurors.

When it was argued that to exclude those who opposed death, and to include only those who supported death, was fundamentally unfair, as the latter were more 'conviction-prone', the US Supreme Court, in the case *Lockhart v McCree* said such a claim was of no constitutional significance.

Once upon a time, politicians promised jobs and benefits to constituents, like 'a chicken in every pot', to get elected.

It was a sure-fire vote getter.

No longer.

Today the lowest level politico up to the president use another sure-fire gimmick to guarantee victory.

Death.

Promise death and the election is yours.

Guaranteed.

Vraiment.

A 'Vote for Hell' in the 'Land of Liberty', with its over one million prisoners, is the ticket to victory. ❏

© *Mumia Abu-Jamal, February 1995*

For further information on Mumia Abu-Jamal, contact Equal Justice, USA at PO Box 5206, Hyattsville, MD 20782; tel 301-699-0042, fax 301-864-2182, e-mail Quixote@igc.apc.
Live from Death Row, *a collection of essays by Mumia Abu-Jamal, will be published by Addison Wesley in April*

Hamilton County Jail, Ohio: waiting for life or death

HUGO BEDAU

Continued from page 113

fairness: putting prosecution and defence on an equal footing. But the basis of the criminal justice system in the USA, at least in theory, has been to give the benefit of the doubt to the defence: the presumption of innocence not a presumption of guilt. Victim-impact statements at the sentencing phase of capital trials are changing that.

Perhaps the most troubling, even laughable, if it weren't so serious, spectacle in the whole politicisation of the death penalty in the USA is the behaviour of the US Congress. Congress is in a funny position: congressmen have to be re-elected every two years, senators every six years but most of the crimes that worry the American public have nothing to do with federal law, they have to do with state law. It's hard to violate federal law and be subject to the death penalty. Not any more. Congress has finally discovered a way to show the American public that it, too, can be tough on crime. Its solution is to make into federal crimes what had hitherto been exclusively state crimes. The Crime Bill was finally enacted in summer 1994, so there are now overlapping state and federal jurisdictions with the result that federal claims take priority over state claims and any number of crimes that would have been prosecuted by the state district attorneys are now subject to prosecution by federal attorneys. Tagged with the old Republican accusation that Democrats are soft on crime, President Clinton made it a high priority to get the Crime Bill through Congress and it is, perhaps, the only piece of important general legislation he has succeeded so far in getting passed. It is more symbolic than important, demonstrating that Democrats can be as tough on crime as their Republican opponents.

I see no prospects for change: politicians in America support capital punishment because they have to be seen by the electorate and by their opponents to be doing something about crime, something visible, something sharp, something memorable, something everybody can understand. Either they don't know how to reduce crime, or they have plausible hypotheses that would — except they know that these measures will cost money and require shifts in priorities that the electorate won't tolerate or that their opponents will exploit to advantage. I cannot see how to raise the quality of political debate in a society that has corrupted its understanding of its own problems to the extent that was demonstrated so clearly in the most recent election. ❏

GREG BLOCHE & BALVIR KAPIHL

Impermissible evidence

An ethical dialogue. Dr Greg Bloche, a psychiatrist and professor at Georgetown University law school, and co-author of Breach of Trust, *and Dr Balvir Kapihl, chief physician at the Virginia Department of Corrections, discuss the physician's role in a prisoner's final moments.* Breach of Trust[1], *a recent report by a coalition of medical and human rights groups, argues that physicians who take part in executions are violating the fundamental ethical principles of medicine. Dr Kapihl has taken part in a dozen executions*

Dr K We use the electric chair in Virginia, and I do not 'take part' in the executions. I'm not involved with the actual execution, the planning or setting up, or anything like that. My role is strictly confined to coming in after it is over and doing an examination and pronouncing death.

I'm in the building, but in another part: I cannot even see the whole thing. They wait about three or four minutes (after they turn the electricity off). And then the officer comes and asks me to enter the chamber. Then I examine the patient and pronounce dead. I turn to the warden and I say: 'This man has expired.'

I do not think my role is inconsistent with [the Hippocratic Oath, which says I will practice 'only for the good of my patients'] because I'm not involved with the execution in any way. Incidentally, the American Medical Association passed a resolution several years ago which says that physicians may not take part in any execution except to pronounce death.

Over 30 years, I have seen people who have been shot dead, stabbed to death, who have committed suicide, and I have prounounced them dead in the emergency room. I've had no more to do with those antecedents — the stabbings and the shootings — than I had to do with the electrocution.

Dr B The American Medical Association (AMA) and other groups have held that to pronounce death is to participate impermissively. Over the last couple of years the definition of participation has been refined. The current position of the AMA and the other groups is that pronouncement of death is unethical.

Here's the central problem. When you go into the death chamber after electricity has been administered, you play a role which isn't merely symbolic, it's central: the determination of whether the execution will continue. Should the individual you evaluate still be alive, then

USA July 1917: pronouncing death

the immediate consequence of your determination is that the execution continues. Another jolt of electricity is administered.

When you're in the emergency room and you determine that someone who you evaluate is still alive, then all the resources of that emergency room and that hospital are marshalled at your command to preserve that patient's life in full compliance with the Hippocratic tradition. Where the Hippocratic tradition is violated in the execution chamber is that your determination, if the person is still alive, will lead to his or her execution.

Dr K There is a small theoretical possibility of that, but the way things actually are, that's a very, very hypothetical question.

Dr B It's not hypothetical. *Breach of Trust* documents how, in a whole series of states, this has happened.

Dr K I agree this is possible, but I think the probability of this happening approaches zero.

Dr B It would not be right for physicians to say merely: 'We don't want to get our hands dirty, and so we don't want to be involved,' and that's the end of the story. The ethical concern here arises from the primary thing that physicians do, which is to take care of patients often at times when patients are in moments of extremis and desperation.

And a critical question becomes, how trustworthy will the doctor be in the eyes of the patient? And if doctors are perceived widely and publicly as serving this function — this lethal function on behalf of the state, not the patient — then this risks undermining the therapeutic credibility of doctors, and the efficacy of doctors both as curers and as comforters.

When the average person approaches doctors and finds them to be strangers, different from the doctor he or she works with, then a vision of what the whole profession does becomes more important in shaping an individual's expectations.

And for prisoners especially, there's often a lot of blurring in their understanding of the roles of physicians: fear on the part of prisoners that the doctor who purports to be ministering to their needs may, in fact, have something far more negative in mind for them.

Dr K Yes, I do see a problem, and I have made up my mind that if my government requires me to do anything more than pronounce death in the manner in which I already have done, I shall refuse. If, for example, the legislature in Virginia passes a law giving a prisoner an option of either the electric chair or a lethal injection. I don't think it has been signed by the governor yet, but we expect that it will be. When that happens, I'm going to send a memorandum to all nurses and physicians that they shall not take part in preparing the medication or the solutions or starting IVs [intravenous injections] and so on. I think that would be direct involvement. I will have no choice but to absolutely, flatly refuse.

Dr K There is [still] a dilemma, and I don't think we've resolved it: the rare probability that an electrocution may not have been successful. Then I would be torn between my medical duty as a professional to start resuscitation and my other duty which is to turn around and tell the warden to take additional measures. Frankly, I do not know which way I shall go if that happens.

Dr B This report and the pronouncements of medical and human rights organisations gives Dr Kapihl an important tool. He can now go back to his superiors, and to the Virginia state legislature, and say: 'A profession that is in some measure self-governing with respect to ethics has taken this very strong stand. Human rights organisations have taken this strong stand as well. And this should weigh on you, my superiors, in determining the orders that you give to me, in determining whether you want to continue to require doctors to be present in the execution chamber and to pronounce death.'

Dr Kapihl is being very courageous and candid in reflecting publicly on the dilemmas that he faces. What we're doing here is empowering him and empowering other prison physicians, who perhaps don't have the courage that Dr Kapihl has, to step forward publicly, to reflect upon this, and to go back to their superiors and their state legislatures and say: 'Stop asking us to do this. This is wrong.'

Dr K I agree and we are going to take a very hard look at it. I'm going to talk to my colleagues, not only in Virginia but in other state departments of corrections, and we will come up with some kind of an action plan.

Dr B One other point. This empowers Dr Kapihl and his colleagues in another way. Should any of these prison superiors seek to discipline Dr Kapihl or his colleagues for saying no when they're asked to pronounce, these organisations can stand publicly and strongly behind Dr Kapihl when he says no.

Dr K I never thought of the remote possibility of a failure of the equipment. I knew in the back of my head that it's a possibility, but to my mind the probability was near vanishing point.

The first time I was involved it was a disturbing experience, it's difficult to recapture the thoughts I had. I was driving back to Richmond and I was filled with a lot of mixed emotions about what I had just done, or had observed. But in Virginia, the people have expressed their views and the death penalty is legal and is the law. ❏

© *'All things considered': National Public Radio, 3 April 1994*

[1] Breach of Trust: Physician Participation in Executions in the United States *(American College of Physicians, Human Rights Watch, National Coalition to Abolish the Death Penalty, Physicians for Human Rights, March 1994)*

RICHARD DIETER

Misspent millions

Despite the exorbitant costs of capital punishment, America feels less safe. Badly needed resources are diverted from effective crime fighting strategies and social programmes — but the politicians don't let on

In 1993 a federally-funded study, conducted at Duke University and one of the most comprehensive analyses on the cost of the death penalty, brought a new perspective to the cost debate. Its authors concluded that capital cases cost at least an extra US$2.16 million per execution, compared to what taxpayers would have spent if defendants were tried without the death penalty and sentenced to life in prison. Moreover, the bulk of those costs occur at the trial level.

Applying these figures on a national level implies that over $200 million was spent just for US executions in the past three years. Yet the national concern about crime indicates that few feel safer for the expense.

In Florida, a budget crisis resulted in the early release of 3,000 prisoners. In Texas, prisoners were serving only 20 per cent of their time and rearrests were common. Georgia laid off 900 correctional personnel and New Jersey has had to dismiss 500 police officers. Yet these same states, and many others like them, are pouring millions of dollars into the death penalty with no resultant reduction in crime.

Before the Los Angeles riots, California had little money for innovations like community policing, but was managing to spend an extra $90 million a year on capital punishment. Texas, with 400 people on death row, is spending an estimated $2.3 million per case, but its murder rate remains one of the highest in the country.

The death penalty is escaping the decisive cost-benefit analysis under which every other government programme is being examined. Rather than being posed as a single, but costly, choice in a spectrum of approaches to crime, the death penalty operates at the extremes of political rhetoric. It is much more expensive than its closest alternative — life imprisonment with no parole. Capital trials are longer and more expensive at every step than other murder trials. Pre-trial motions, expert witness investigations, jury selection and the necessity for two trials — one on guilt and one on sentencing — make capital cases extremely costly, even before the appeals process begins. Guilty pleas are almost unheard of when the punishment is death. In addition, many of these trials result in a life sentence rather than the death penalty, so the state pays the cost of life imprisonment on top of the expensive trial.

The high price of the death penalty is often most keenly felt in small counties responsible for both the prosecution and defence of capital defendants. A single trial can mean near bankruptcy, tax increases and the laying-off of vital personnel. Trials costing a county $100,000 from unbudgeted funds are common; some officials have even gone to jail for resisting payment.

There have been numerous indications from other areas of the country that the death penalty is straining the budgets of state and local governments and that the financial drain is getting worse.

• In San Diego, California, the prosecution costs alone (not counting defence costs or appeals) for three capital cases averaged over half a million dollars each. One estimate puts the total Californian death penalty expense bill at $1 billion since 1977. California has executed two people during that time, one of whom refused to appeal his case.

• In Jasper County, Mississippi, the circuit judge and the district attorney had to address the county supervisors to get more money for death penalty prosecutions. The only solution was to raise county taxes. 'It's going to be a fairly substantial increase,' said the board president, John Sims. 'I hope the taxpayers understand...'

• In Connecticut, a state with only a handful of death row inmates, *The Connecticut Law Tribune* was unable to calculate the total costs of capital punishment but concluded that the 'costs are staggering.' State's attorney Mark Solak said he spent between 1,000 and 1,500 hours preparing one capital prosecution. The defence attorney in the case noted that if his client had been given an offer of life in prison without parole he would have accepted it 'in a heartbeat'. 'The case,' he said, 'would have been over in 15 minutes. No-one would have spent a penny.'

• In South Carolina, the *Sun News* reported that the bills for death penalty cases are 'skyrocketing' because of a State Supreme Court ruling that attorneys in death penalty cases deserve reasonable fees. Before the decision, attorneys received no more than $2,500 for each death penalty case.

• In Harris County, Texas, there were recently 135 pending death penalty cases. State Judge Miron Love estimated that if the death penalty is assessed in just 20 per cent of these cases, it will cost the taxpayers a minimum of $60 million. Judge Love, who oversees the county's courts, remarked: 'We're running the county out of money.'

There have been many similar reactions from state and local officials who question the wisdom of spending such exorbitant sums on such unpredictable and isolated cases. In Tennessee, the number of people sentenced to death has dropped because prosecutors say death penalty cases cost too much.

In Texas, Judge Doug Shaver of Houston was concerned about the high costs of so many capital cases: 'I can't figure out why our county is prosecuting so many more (death) cases than comparably large counties around Texas. When the law changed so defendants can be sentenced to 40 years flat time (as

Continued on page 126

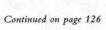
Can't afford a big fancy lawyer? don't worry there are . . . .

loopholes

PHILIP WILSON

MICHAEL L RADELET

Race and death

When the Supreme Court threw out all existing death penalty laws in 1972, it did so in large part because of the arbitrariness and racism involved in capital punishment. Between 1930 and 1967, there were 3,859 people executed in America, of whom 54 per cent were black. Racism was particularly evident in rape cases: here 405 of the 455 men put to death were black. Among those executed during that period for murder, 51 per cent were black. Today, 50 per cent of those on death row are black or another minority. In short, all the refinements in death sentencing that have occurred in the last 23 years in America — refinements that were supposed to make the system more fair — have resulted in a one per cent decrease in the proportion of minorities subject to execution. Racism in American death sentencing is alive and well.

Recent research has found that the race of the victim is far more important than the race of the defendant in predicting who is sentenced to death. The most sophisticated study, *Equal Justice and the Death Penalty: A Legal and Empirical Analysis* (Northeastern University Press, 1990), done in Georgia by David Baldus and his colleagues, found that the odds of a death sentence for those who kill whites were 4.3 times higher than for those who killed blacks. These patterns held even after Baldus considered some 230 variables that might explain the disparities on non-racial grounds. Even among those who killed strangers, or among those who killed during the commission of other felonies (for example, robbery or rape), those who killed whites were treated more severely. The criminal justice system functions at full speed only when higher status people are victimised.

In the 1987 case of *McCleskey v Georgia*, the US Supreme Court, in a 5-4 decision, acknowledged the legitimacy of the Baldus data, but said, in effect, 'It just doesn't matter.' The Court held that before it would intervene in a capital case on race grounds, the defendant would have to show *intentional* racial bias *in his individual case*. Unless prosecutors overtly state that there are racial motives behind the decision to seek death in a given case, capital defendants are left without a claim. In 1993, the author of that decision, retired Justice Lewis Powell, stated it was the worst decision he had ever made. On 25 September 1991, Warren McCleskey was executed.

Americans are well-aware that the death penalty is biased by class and race; a 1991 Gallup Poll found that 45 per cent of a national sample agreed with the statement 'A black person is more likely than a white person to receive the death penalty for the same crime.' Sixty per cent believed that the poor were more likely than the rich to be condemned to death for the same crime. The conclusion is clear. Americans love the death penalty so much that the fact that it is racist does not seem to matter. Given the history and reality of racism in America, in fact, one could argue that the death penalty's racism is a pro-death penalty argument, not an abolitionist argument. ❏

Race of defendants executed

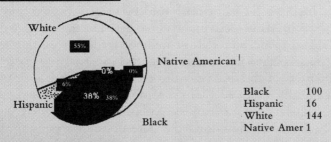

Black	100
Hispanic	16
White	144
Native Amer	1

Race of death row inmates: Half are minorities

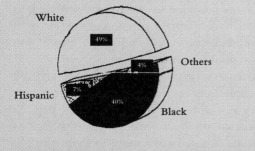

Black	1180
Hispanic	205
White	1446
Others	117

Total: 2,948
(October 1994)
*All death row figures
are from the NAACP
Legal Defense Fund*

Race of victims: Almost all capital cases involve white victims

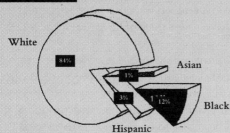

About 85% of the victims in death penalty cases are white, even though 50% of murder victims are black

*Persons executed for
interracial murders*

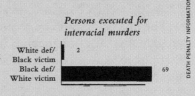

White def/
Black victim   2
Black def/
White victim   69

DEATH PENALTY INFORMATION CENTER

Continued from page 123

an alternative to death), and when you start taking into account what the taxpayers are getting for their money, it seems like some defendants should be tried...without the death penalty.'

Former Texas Attorney General Jim Mattox agrees: 'Life without parole could save millions of dollars.' 'In other words' he wrote, 'it's cheaper to lock 'em up and throw away the key... As violent crime continues to escalate, it's something to consider.'

California has been hit particularly hard by natural disasters and the economic recession. Many social programmes have had to be cut. Yet the state continues to spend hundreds of millions of dollars on the death penalty which has resulted in two executions in 17 years.

Even supporters of the death penalty recognise that it is a financial loser. In financially strapped Orange County, Vanda Bresnan, who manages the criminal courts, remarked: 'Even though I do believe in the death penalty, I wonder how long the state or county can afford it.' Defence attorney Gary Proctor, who practices in the same county, believes that the solution will be found by cutting other services. 'What I see happening is that other services provided to the taxpayer — such as libraries and parks — will be cut back. Certain people are not aware of the trade-offs.' He added: 'Strong beliefs are easy enough to hold if you don't think they're coming out of your pocket.'

In rural Kentucky, tax bases are small and budgets are already stretched. When an expensive capital case is about to be heard in court, the state and county often argue for weeks about who will pay. As Michael Mager, executive director of the Kentucky County Judge-Executives Association, points out: 'A little rural county in Kentucky just can't deal with bills like that.'

And in Connecticut, the chief state's attorney, John M Bailey, echoed similar concerns. 'Every dollar we spend on a capital case is a dollar we can't spend anywhere else... We have to let the public know what it costs' to pursue a capital case.

As the actual costs of capital punishment become clearer, the public will be in a better position to judge the death penalty as they would other programmes. If a programme is highly cost intensive, given to years of litigious expense, focused on only a few individuals, and produces no measurable results, then it should be replaced by better alternatives. ❏

VLADIMIR SELEDTSOV

GHAZI RABIHAVI

White rock

The photographer jumped down over the gallows and his three
cameras jumped around with him. We were worried something
might happen to them. The gallows were still lying on the floor of the
pick-up truck. He dusted off his trousers and said:

'Are you kids from around here?'

We looked at each other and one of us said:

'Are you going to take pictures of us or the dead man?'

The photographer blinked nervously and asked:

'Is he dead?' and ran, complete with the solid looking black cameras,
to the patrol car. It had arrived with these three *pasdars** carrying G-3
guns about an hour earlier. And one of us had said:

'I bet those guns aren't loaded.'

Two of the officers threw their guns onto the back seat of the car and
walked over to the pick-up. And one of us had said then:

'I bet those guns are loaded.'

They began to help take out the gallows posts from the truck and to set them up on either side of the white rock where they had already dug two shallow holes to support them. Before they had found the rock, one of the *pasdars* had asked us:

'Hey, you. Can any of you get us a stool?' and one of us had said:

'He's going to be hanged, isn't he? Because you have to hang him.' But the other guy said:

'Don't bother with a stool: this white rock will do.'

A few local men were coming our way from different parts of the town. It was a good Friday morning for a hanging, only it would have been even better if it hadn't started to snow, or if we'd had gloves. They said if it snowed they wouldn't hang him. It wasn't snowing when they brought the dead man. When they brought him he was alive.

He came out of the ambulance and sniffed the air. He had pulled up the zipper of his grey and green jumper — or someone had done it up for him because his hands were strapped behind his back. The first snowflakes settled on his hair. A group of locals ran towards him. The photographer was checking out his cameras. The headlights of the ambulance had been left on. The snowflakes were light and soft. They melted even before they touched the lights. One of us said:

'Pity. I wasn't even born when they executed the Shah's guard.' One of us answered:

'My brother was born then; my dad sat him up on his shoulders so he could see the guy being executed. Bang! Bang!'

The truck driver said:

'I'd love to stay and watch. It'd mean a blessing for me. But I've got to deliver this food for the troops.' The fat *pasdar* scratched his beard with the gun barrel and said:

'Good luck.' The truck driver ran to the pick-up cursing the snow.

The prisoner was pacing up and down in the snow without any idea that he was moving closer and closer to the gallows. Sometimes, he just stood there, with his long, thin legs, turning his head this way and that, snuffing the air. He wrinkled his nose and waggled his eyebrows, trying to shift the blindfold to find out where he was. But the blindfold was too tight. One of us said:

'Shout out his name so he knows where he is.' Another said:

'When I used to know his name he was a different person.'

INDEX ON CENSORSHIP
33 Islington High Street
London N1 9BR
United Kingdom

BUSINESS REPLY MAIL
FIRST CLASS PERMIT NO.7796 NEW YORK, NY

Postage will be paid by addressee.

INDEX ON CENSORSHIP
c/o Fund for Free Expression
485 Fifth Avenue
NEW YORK, NY   10164-0709

A couple of people were still working on trying to get the gallows firm in the ground. Only men and children could come to watch. One of the guys, who had been given a leg up on the cupped hands of another, jumped down and said:

'Where's the other one?' The prisoner turned his head and said:

'Yeah. Where is he?' We didn't know the other guy; he wasn't from our town. We only saw him once — no, it was twice — on the same night. It was the beginning of autumn. The sun was just setting when we saw him entering the gates. He had a long turtle-neck sweater pulled down over his trousers. His clothes were black; like his hair. The officer on the gate was eating meat and rice. The stranger was carrying a bouquet of pink roses, and he was trying to hide a black plastic bag

underneath it. He didn't like us watching him. But we did anyway and worked out that there were two bottles in the bag. He had the address of the prisoner but didn't know which way to go. So we showed him. At first, we thought he was a rather tall boxer. He ran his fingers through his hair and lifted his head. Then he looked down at us from under his eyelids. His eyebrows were shaved across his nose where they should have run together and he smiled at us. The sun trembling through the

VLADIMIR SELEDTSOV

plane tree spalahed his face with light and shade. He smiled and turned in the direction we had pointed. The security guy was washing his plate under the tap and asked us:

'Who was that?' and we told him. He looked over to the prisoner's house.

People were moving closer to the gallows, gathering in front of it. The photographer was sitting in the ambulance having a smoke. The prisoner, walking towards the gallows, was still unaware of where he was. One of the guards took his arm and pulled him over to the rock. The photographer grabbed his cameras and jumped out of the ambulance. He was wearing one of those safari vests with lots of pockets. He got out a wire contraption from one of them and hooked them onto the shoulder tabs. Then he got out some white cloth and stretched it over the frame he had made. Now the snow wouldn't bother him. He ran across to the gallows with the umbrella that had sprouted from his shoulder.

None of the spectators were related to the prisoner; we didn't know if he had any relations. He was a loner; he built the wooden bodies for stringed instruments and twice a week went out of town. People said he had a wife and children somewhere that he had abandoned. The grocer had said to him:

'Give it another chance. You're only 45. It's just the right time to get married.' The prisoner had smiled and said:

'Just the right time.'

The guy holding onto the prisoner's arm was still looking at the hanging rope. Then he told the prisoner:

'Stand on top of this stone, will you, pal. Just to test everything's OK.'

The prisoner's feet searched for the stone. Found it. If we could have seen his eyes, we could have told if he was frightened or not. That midnight, in the autumn, when the guards attacked his house and arrested both of them, he pressed his face against the rear window of the car, his eyes searching everywhere for his lover. Then, his voice trembling, he yelled from behind the glass:

'Leave him alone!' The car drove off; a crushed pink rose was still sticking to the back tyre.

The prisoner asked:

'Is it time?' The *pasdar* said:

'No. The *hadji*[*] hasn't arrived yet. We can't start without him.' He said:

'Then what?' The officer said:

'Take your shoes off. This is only a trial run.' The prisoner took his bare feet out of the loose-fitting canvas shoes and stood on them. His long, thin toes were red with cold. They had up-ended the white rock and were holding it in position; the slightest kick would topple it, leaving his feet dangling in space. The *pasdar* said:

'Now climb up.' He put one foot on the rock. It shifted, swayed, nearly fell over. The guard jumped forward and set it straight again.

'What's with you? Are you in a hurry?' he said. Then he got up and, one by one, carefully placed the prisoner's feet on the stone. The prisoner stood on the stone and was raised up above the crowd. His shoes were left below, on the ground, and everything around him was white: the sky, the snow. The rest of the officers and the driver were standing under a big umbrella like you have on a beach, next to the patrol car. It was a long way from the gallows. The photographer said:

'What are you doing? *Hadji* isn't here yet.' The guard said:

'No, he isn't.' The photographer said:

'Then come over here and have some saffron dates.' The guard said;

'Only if you let me stand under your umbrella,' and burst out laughing. The photographer looked up at his umbrella and said:

'It's for the cameras,' and walked towards the patrol car. The spectators were not saying anything. They were just standing there, silent, looking at the prisoner. Hanging onto one side of the gallows, the guard pulled himself up next to him. If he hadn't been wearing boots, there would have been enough room for another pair of feet. The stone wobbled again, but didn't fall over. The guard grabbed the hanging rope and struggled to get it round the prisoner's neck. The prisoner was trying to help, but couldn't see what the other guy was doing. Then he jumped down and the rock stayed firm. He said:

'Now you see how steady it is?'

In the distance a car was approaching. One of the *pasdars* called out:

'Hurry up!' He looked at the patrol car and then at the prisoner and said:

'Try to get used to it, then, when the time comes, you won't panic.' The only movement in the landscape was the distant car. We could only just see it, but because of the whiteness of the snow, we could make out what make it was: either a Mercedes or a Hillman. *Hadji* must have been lounging in the back seat. The guard said:

'Make sure it doesn't work loose. I'll be right back.' The prisoner said:

'What?' But the guard had already moved off to the patrol car. The boot of the approaching car sagged low to the ground from the weight on the back seat. It drew nearer to where we were, but it was still a good way off. The guards were still eating their dates near the patrol car. Women were not allowed to watch because this was not their business: it had nothing to do with them. The prisoner tried to shift the rock with his feet. It refused to move. One of the spectators jumped forward but quickly froze to the spot. All of us were waiting for the approaching car. The *pasdars* and the photographer were throwing the date stones into the snow. The snowflakes were melting as they hit the ground. The prisoner again tried to shift the rock. It moved; but didn't fall. The silent spectators stood stock still as if they were frozen to the spot and it wasn't snowing. Our hands were red with cold. Red as the wine the guards found in the prisoner's house the night of his arrest. One of the bottles was empty; the other still half full. The guards also took the two long-stemmed crystal glasses. By now we could see the car. It was a Hillman. One of the officers threw the date box away. The rest quickly ate up what they had left in their hands. One of the *pasdars* went to meet the car and the rest followed. The photographer glanced at the gallows. He started to move closer, but changed his mind and walked over to the ambulance instead. The prisoner was kicking at the rock with his feet. It tottered, fell down and left his bare feet hanging in the air. His long, thin toes were searching for the stone. But by then it was too late. Then the movement stopped and his feet hung motionless. The car finally arrived dazzling us with its headlights. We went to warm our hands at the headlights of the ambulance because that was what the photographer was doing. ❏

Tehran 1994

Translated by Neda Jalali
* Pasdar: *revolutionary guard;* Hadji: *one who has been to Mecca; here, a mullah*

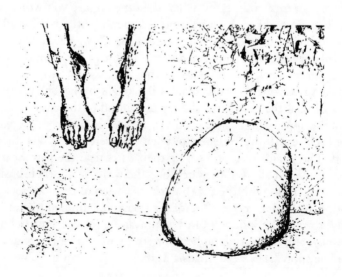

VLADIMIR SELEDTSOV

ALEXANDER SOLZHENITSYN

J HAILLOT/CAMERA PRESS

Let the Chechen go

Alexander Solzhenitsyn's views on the invasion of Chechnya have not endeared him to government nor critics in Russia. Natalia Zhelnorova of *Argumenty i fakty* asks him for some clarification

INTERVIEW

NZ: Aleksandr Isaevich, what are your thoughts as you watch the Chechnyan slaughter?

The military offensive against Chechnya was a grave error. Quite apart from our evident lack of military talent, and irrespective of the outcome, it will be particularly damaging to our relations with the Caucasus and the Muslim world.

This offensive should have been avoided at all cost. The Chechen crisis is being treated as though it were something confined to December 1994 and January 1995. This is a distortion of the facts. Government, deputies, the public and the press are trying to cover up their blunders. This sore has festered for three years, and neither the presidential team, nor successive governments, nor the old Supreme Soviet, nor the present Parliament, nor the media, nor the public have lifted a finger to resolve the crisis.

Three years ago, Dudayev declared Chechnya's independence. He did it illegally, with no public mandate, and certainly without the support of two-thirds of the electorate as would normally be expected. And did our executive and legislative powers react? Did the public react? No. It all began in those three years: the killings, the robbery, the violence against Russians who were hounded out of their homes and out of Chechnya itself. The terror spread, first to the Mineralnye Vody region, then to the Northern Caucasus and, finally, to Moscow. Whole trainloads of goods disappeared, billions of roubles were stolen. The perpetrators of these crimes took refuge in newly independent Chechnya. And so the sore festered. Something had to be done. Not a single one of our human rights activists went to talk to the hapless Russian families who were being dispossessed of their homes. Not a single cameraman chose to go and photograph the weeping, homeless women. Worse still, after Chechnya had declared independence, our government subsidised it while Russian territories (*oblasti*) footed the bill.

Some see you as a supporter of the Chechen war.

That's astonishing. During the course of my trip across Russia, I repeatedly said that Chechnya should be given independence. But the Moscow media were determined to ignore my statements. I also spoke about Tajikistan. Now Chechnya is ablaze and everyone is asking: 'Why is Solzhenitsyn silent?' When Tajikistan explodes, they'll say the same. Which is why I am issuing yet another warning: we must leave Tajikistan without further delay.

When Dudayev declared independence we should have acted right away: strengthened our borders, organised customs posts to prevent the passage of drugs or arms. We should have declared all Chechens in Russia foreigners and asked them either to go home or get a visa, like any other foreigner... And we should have provided refuge for all Russians who wanted to leave Chechnya.

I suggested this to our leaders two-and-a-half years ago, while I was still in Vermont [USA]. It would have been a salutary lesson for Chechnya. 'By all means, build your Great Chechnya', I said. 'If you want international recognition, go out and get it. If you want diplomatic relations, send out your 50 ambassadors and open as many houses in Grozny to receive foreign diplomats. Build an air force. Do everything you need to do.' There is just one thing: when the Communists were distributing Russian lands to all and sundry, they gave away the Cossack lands on the left bank of the river Terek to Chechnya. These lands should not be recognised as Chechen territory.

You proposed independence for Chechnya, but politicians didn't want to be answerable for the collapse, not just of the USSR, but of Russia.

They should have broken out of the constrictions of traditional military and diplomatic thought. Russia isn't the only place that wants to hold on to what it's got. England and France have applied the same principle for centuries; today the USA is doing the same in a modified form. But we should know how to step out of this strait-jacket.

You will be accused of wanting to destroy Russia.

When one part of the body is gangrenous, it has to be amputated to save the rest. The integrity of Russia is more important. I have heard it said that our leadership is ready to agree to a confederation with Chechnya. In fact we need neither a confederation nor a federation. The Russian Federation is an artificial, Leninist invention. Russia never was a federation; it never was formed on the basis of a union of ready-made states. Today the autonomous republics are based almost entirely on minorities. The 1989 census shows that Tataria has a Tatar population of 48.5 per cent; Yakutia is 37 per cent Yakut; Bashkiria 22 per cent Bashkir; and Karelia just 10 per cent Karelian. It is only in Chechnya, Tuva and Chuvashia that the indigenous population is over two-thirds of the population as a whole [and, since June 1992, Ingushetia]. In the remaining republics Lenin's formula has given power to a minority.

And what are the central authorities doing? They have signed agreements with Tataria and Bashkiria which make a mockery of the Russian state. Power should never come through ethnic privilege. Article 74 of the Criminal Code of the Russian Federation specifies that to accord any kind of privileged status to citizens on a racial or ethnic basis is an infringement of criminal legislation. Yet that is exactly what is happening. Russians are being forced out of Bashkiria, Tataria and elsewhere because of their ethnic status. Let us be consistent: either we keep to our Criminal Code or we behave like a real federation.

Chechnya should have been allowed to learn from experience. Perhaps then it would have come back to Russia of its own accord. Its only alternative is to be forced violently into union with the Turkish empire, through Georgia. Today, a small nation cannot survive as a state. In the twentieth century the strength of states is being consolidated worldwide.

I raised this issue four-and-a-half years ago in my article 'Rebuilding Russia'. Small nations can break away, if that's what they want. But it's unrealistic; they won't create a state.

There was an assembly in Cheboksary recently, where the leaders of autonomous republics from the Volga region made utopian proposals that would lead directly to Russia's collapse. These leaders do not even represent the national majorities of their republics. One proposal is to restore the Council of the Heads of Republics. But they already form part of the Council of the Russian Federation, together with the leaders of the autonomous regions (*krai*) and the autonomous territories (*oblasti*). They propose that autonomous republics should take precedence over the regions and territories. Moreover, they want to create a Congress of the Peoples of Russia. It's sheer madness. There are over a hundred ethnic groups in Russia. If every nation is represented by a single vote, this will put Russia in the same position as a tiny nation of 500 people. They are not planning to give the Russians four-fifths of the votes that they would be entitled to on a proportional basis.

We refused to acknowledge Chechnya as an independent state while it was in a position of strength. Are we to do it now that we have bombed and killed?

Military action creates a terrible impasse. The post-war situation will be difficult in the extreme. If we were to subordinate Chechnya, we'd cause civil war across the Caucasus and spark off hostility with the Islamic world. The significance of the Muslim world in the next century will be huge. It is a growing force. There is only one superpower left in the world; it's their headache. Under no circumstances should we enter into conflict with the Muslim world in our present sickly state, with so many sicknesses of our own to contend with. ❏

Translated by Irena Maryniak from the interview first published in Argumenty i fakty *1-2 and 3 in January 1995*

MINORITIES

GÖRAN OLLSSON

DAVRELL TIEN

Chechen imbroglio

Russia's war in Chechnya has a long history. But Moscow has learned no lessons and the Chechen are fighting on

Despite a population of only one million, the Chechens have played a catalytic role in Russian history. As Solzhenitsyn describes them in the *Gulag Archipelago*, the Chechens were the only nation that militantly refused to accept the Soviet psychology of submission. 'No Chechen ever tried to be of service or to please the authorities. Their attitude towards them was proud and even hostile.' Moreover, notes Solzhenitsyn, 'the strange thing was that everybody feared them and no-one prevented them from living as they liked.'

Chechen-Russian relations over the last two centuries shows both nations defining themselves in terms of their willingness and ability to make war upon one another. Pushkin, Lermontov and Tolstoy were at once stimulated and perplexed by their country's role as the aggressor. All three pay tribute to the spirit of Chechen resistance in their work.

Early in his literary career, Alexander Pushkin found inspiration for *Prisoner of the Caucasus* — the verse tale of a Russian officer held prisoner

Outside Grozny, February 1995: the war goes to the villages

by the mountaineers — in the figure of General Aleksei Ermolov, the tsarist commander who pioneered genocide to win military victory. By massacring civilian villagers Ermolov sought to impress would-be rebels. 'I desire that my name should guard our frontiers more potently than chains of fortresses, that my word should be for the natives a law more inevitable than death.' The poem, which won the immediate admiration of readers in St Petersburg, made the Caucasus a well of literary inspiration in the minds of Russians.

In reality relations between the two peoples were less romantic. Mikhail Lermontov, who also saw military action in the Caucasus, composed a poem depicting a Chechen slinking along the bank of the Terek river, honing his dagger to kill a Russian child. His lines became a favourite Russian lullaby. In his novel *A Hero of Our Time*, the Chechens are described as unkempt, homicidal psychopaths. Lermontov's hero, a Russian officer who commits crimes against the local people to relieve his cynical ennui, is punished only by his own bad conscience. Tolstoy and Lermontov perceived the savage hypocrisy of their country's claims to be spreading European civilisation and justice, but did not question the right of empire.

The Caucasians also had their poets. For half a century after his capture the bards sang about Chechen rebel leader Sheikh Mansur who 'was born to tread the Moscoff's pride down to the lowly dust; he fought, he conquered, near and wide, that northern race accursed...'

If Chechen literary accomplishments are less known and developed, it is due in part at least to the physical elimination of writers and potential writers. In Soviet times writers were frequently interrupted by arrest, imprisonment and assassination. Hassan Israilov, a poet and journalist who satirised the plundering of Chechnya by Communist officials, abandoned poetry for politics. In 1940 he led an armed insurrection, convinced that the drives against so many different social groups (kulak, mullah, bandit, bourgeois-nationalist) were a step-by-step plan to destroy the nation as a whole. Israilov's leadership sparked a wave of successful uprisings against the local Bolsheviks, leading to the establishment of a provisional Chechen-Ingush government. The peoples of the Caucasus have had a well-developed anti-colonialist sentiment since the early nineteenth century when Sufi leaders such as Ghazi Muhammad preached: 'A Muslim cannot be a slave or subject to anyone, nor can he pay tribute to anyone, not even to another Muslim. He who is a Muslim must be a free man, and there must be equality among all Muslims.'

When Ghazi Muhammad was cornered and bayoneted to death in 1831, Sheikh Shamil succeeded him as military and political leader. Shamil, who successfully held off the tsarist military for decades, became famous throughout Europe; observers, including Karl Marx, followed the Caucasian struggle sympathetically. Today, in the West at least, Islamic revolution is associated with intolerance and fanaticism. But the usual portrayal of Shamil is of a heroic figure who organised primitive tribal peoples desperately fighting for their lives. Islam was the only banner under which the linguistically distinct ethnic groups could unify.

But an independent North Caucasus state was not to be: Russia poured in troops and money to crush it. The number of Russian soldiers increased constantly, from 4,000 men in Tiflis in 1800 to over 200,000 in the 1840s. Then, as now, the disparity of resources made military victory by the Caucasians near impossible.

Some Islamic thinkers in the Caucasus have proposed the path of non-violence as a means of accommodating Russian rule. In the early 1860s, war-weary Chechens were receptive to Kunta Kishiev, a goatherd turned religious philosopher, who preached mystical asceticism, detachment from worldly affairs and 'non-resistance to evil'. The Russian authorities arrested him, and banished him to the mental ward of a Russian prison hospital, where he died three years later.

Given the enormous expense of quartering soldiers in the North Caucasus and the intractable resistance of nations like the Chechens, what motivated Russia to hold on? The literary heritage is certainly a factor. Russia could no more surrender the lands immortalised by Pushkin, Lermontov and Tolstoy than America would surrender the mythic Wild West.

The land of the Caucasus also symbolised freedom for Russian peasants fleeing serfdom to join the Cossacks. For centuries, Moscow supported the Cossacks in their drive to the fertile valleys above the Caucasus mountains, using them in turn to defend its turbulent southern frontier. Lieutenant Gernal A Veliaminov, a contemporary of Ermolov, settled Cossacks among the Caucasians to reduce their ability to grow food.

Control of food production was also a favourite weapon of social control under Soviet rule. The North Caucasus was the first territory in the Soviet Union slated for complete collectivisation of the rural economy and the liquidation of kulaks. When this was announced in 1929 Chechnya erupted and overthrew the Soviet government. Moscow sent messages to say it had been a mistake, and 150 Soviet secret police (GPU) hurried to arrest the leaders of the revolt. The GPU were massacred and an insurrection began. In 1930, after a patchy campaign, the Red Army withdrew. Large quantities of industrial goods, at low prices, flooded the shops; an amnesty was declared. But by 1931 GPU agents swept up 35,000 kulak counter-revolutionaries and religious nationalists ideologists: few were ever seen again.

With war raging as the time for spring planting approaches, it seems inevitable that history will repeat itself and agriculturally self-sufficient Chechnya will face yet another food crisis as a result of Russian military action.

Industry, too, has been a focus of ethnic friction. Around the turn of the century Grozny became a centre for the petroleum industry, attracting an influx of Russian settlers. During the Russian civil war some Chechens made a strategic alliance with the Bolsheviks against the White armies; however, when the Bolsheviks consolidated their rule, the Communist party recruited Russian oil workers. By 1937, there were still only 5,535 Chechen and Ingush employed in Grozny factories. Today control of the oil industry is the object of bitter struggle. When Dudayev turned off the flow of oil to Russia in March 1992, Moscow was forced to share part of the republic's oil revenues, a humiliating and threatening precedent. At the outset of the war, after the bombing of Chechen oil refineries, one of Russia's most senior economic ministers proclaimed the war economically sound because of future oil revenues from the republic. Quelling banditry (or the mafia), Moscow's oft-repeated pretext for military intervention now as then, has little to do with fighting crime and everything to do with economic control.

Seeing Chechen-Russian history as brutal, calculated colonialism is not new, even in Russia. When the Bolsheviks came to power Shamil and the other North Caucasus rebels who fought against the tsars were deemed progressive historical figures by the new Soviet government. In theory the Bolsheviks supported the demands of oppressed minorities; in practice the Red Army troops in the North Caucasus behaved so arrogantly that it took a year, from 1920-1921, to incorporate the North Caucasus into the Soviet state. The war was kept secret.

Chechnya 1995: in the ruins of Grozny

Attempts have even been made to deprive the Chechen of their history. The first target was Shamil, whose status as an anti-colonial hero came under attack in the 1930s. In 1937 the NKVD arrested nearly 14,000 officials and intellectuals in the Chechen-Ingush republic; indigenous Communist leadership was replaced by outsiders. After the war, North Caucasian history was rewritten, transforming Shamil and his fellow rebels into reactionaries.

The deportation of the Chechen and Inguish *en masse* to Siberia and Central Asia in 1944, including those living outside the republic, resulted in the deaths of 30-50 per cent of the population as a result of mistreatment during transportation and internment.

In 1957, after Stalin's death, Chechens and Ingush forced their way back after a 13-year absence. They were told endless lies about the reason for their deportation. The charge of collaboration with the Germans rang false, but new lies were invented, documents forged. According to one such, the deportation by Stalin had whisked the people from certain death at the hands of the German army just in time.

With the advent of *glasnost*, a new generation of Caucasian intellectuals pressed for the rehabilitation of Shamil and the truth about the past. Poet Hussein Satuev declared: 'When lies are written about a nation it dies again. Our people have experienced the hideousness of the personality cult. We are still crying on our stones. Why should we die twice? There must be truth.' In 1988, Moscow relented. Attempts to rehabilitate Chechen Communist heroes failed: only the Sufi leaders would do. Finally, in 1990, the statue of Ermolov was removed from Grozny.

As Russian tanks grind through the Chechen countryside, shooting indiscriminately, it is little wonder that people mistrust Moscow's intentions. Every Chechen boy knows about Shamil; every villager admires Dudayev; and every grandparent tells stories about the men with no beliefs or values who come from time to time to steal and kill and lie. They are, warn the old people, fanatics, it is better to fight them than surrender. ❏

Further reading: The North Caucasus Barrier, *edited by Marie Bennigsen Broxup (Hurst and Company, London, 1992)*
Russia: Three Months of War in Chechnya *(Human Rights Watch/Helsinki, February 1995)*

DIARY

JUDITH VIDAL-HALL

Small war, big deal

Agdash camp: most refugees were absorbed, 60,000 wait to go home, somewhere

3am Sunday 9 October 1994

We bucketed in on the tail of a storm. Long before we could see land, or even the perpetual fires that burned on shore, the white horses whipped up by the storm had turned into a grey spume, like spent chewing-gum. It broke off the top of the waves and rolled across the darkening surface of the sea. As we made our sluggish way towards the dawn and the distant mountains, our wake burned red and green on the darkening water. And when we woke at anchor in the morning — around 3am — the fetid stench turned the stomach.

So this was Baku, object of our journey, 'land of fire' and birthplace of the Zoroastrian god Ahura-Mazda himself. Now, I had read some days before, with oil deposits 'to rival those of Kuwait', and where the holy fires had spurted up from the rocks since the beginning of time a new temple was planned. There had been a time when boomtown Baku produced more oil than the whole of the USA. Great fortunes were made in the nineteenth-century oil rush: Norway's Nobel brothers made their first pile here before going on to bigger booms back home.

We had crossed six seas and gone through three captains in a month to bring food to refugees from Azerbaijan's war with Armenia.

At nights we had battened down the hatches against river pirates on the Volga who circled us in the dark and left our rusting hulk and its dubious cargo intact.

The streets, when we finally walked out of the port into the 'revolution' we had watched on the ship's flickering television, were quiet. There were tanks guarding key government offices, the army was much in evidence but the curfew was more threatened than real, simply another way of extorting money from those who could be forced to pay.

Beyond the guns at the hotel door, a motley crowd of local mafia, senior US and UK oil bosses, equally senior and heavily armed Afghans in close conversation with men in Mercedes, Turkish 'businessmen', Iranian 'students' and Pakistani import-export men gave the lobby a semblance of life and normality. Coup or revolution, no-one was leaving while there was money to be made. But the food was good.

Monday
The sea sparkling in the early morning sun beyond the waterfront and broad, tree-lined boulevards of a pleasant Russian colonial seaside resort. On closer inspection it was covered by a thick layer of black crude oil studded with debris from many lands. Pollution seems irrecoverable. Further out of town, forests of antiquated derricks and clapped-out pumps abandoned to an oily wasteland, stretched for miles.

The promenade was a shallow facade of a town — or towns, there are several quite different and distinct — down on its luck. Independence and new-found nationalism doesn't translate into civic pride. The grand neo-classical Moorish of the Russian colonial town was neglected and crumbling; the narrow lanes of the old town, the commercial heart of the city before it lost its Armenians, were a shadow of themselves. Only up on the citadel behind its massy wall with elegant Persian inscriptions was there solace for the eyes in the glorious architecture of its early Muslim rulers. But even here, the heart had gone out of it: a place done up for the tourists who did not come — and to foster the Islamic identity that alone could make a nation out of seven million people more loyal to village or clan than to a state they did not know and that did less and less for them. Self-appointed guides and scavengers drag the idle stranger down into the cellars of ancient houses. Among mediocre Caucasian rugs and chipped bric-a-brac, there are exquisite icons set in silver, one no larger than a large postage stamp on a broken chain. Only US$20. Too cheap for an Armenian life or death.

Cheap electrical goods, bolts of gaudy cloth and plenty of food for those who could buy it, all from Turkey, fill the shops and spill out onto the streets where stalls with nothing more than two or three packets of cigarettes jostle for space with old women from the villages selling their produce. It all seems oddly transitory: no-one is here for longer than it takes to get out again, gather a stake or do the deal in hand.

The only bookshop in evidence had been taken over by the Turkish Islamists and the best paper in town, sold out everyday, was the Azerbaijan edition of the Islamist paper *Zaman,* printed and edited in Ankara, flown in daily. The shop was packed and bearded young Turks were doing a brisk trade in small practical manuals on *The Meaning of Islam,* how-to-do-it books on prayer, duties, observances and rituals.

I ask how many mosques there are in the city for a population of near 2 million. Iftikar, the beaky young teacher of English looked puzzled. 'To the best of my knowledge and if I am not mistaken, I believe there are three.' From where we stood, high above the city, he could spot only one ugly modern minaret but pointed out the older and far more numerous Armenian churches dotted around below.

Tuesday

When a crowd of hundreds of thousands demonstrated in the centre of Yerevan in February 1988 demanding the immediate annexation of Nagorno-Karabakh — a majority Armenian enclave inside Azerbaijan — by Armenia, retaliatory pogroms against Armenians broke out in Sumgait, an unlovely satellite town 30 kilometers north of Baku.

Hostilities were suspended for a year as Armenia dealt with its earthquake casualties. But almost a year to the day later, in December 1989, the Armenian Supreme Soviet voted to unite with the territory. Within days, Azeri mobs turned on Armenians in Baku. Soviet troops intervened in protests by the main opposition grouping, the Popular Front, and Azeris were killed. Armenians inside Nagorno-Karabakh hunted down Azeri communities and the exodus followed: a near-total exchange of Armenians and Azeris: 500,000, a million?

Thus began the war, the refugee disaster, the rise of the Popular Front and the vicious clan feuding within the political elite that has resulted in three presidents and several attempted coups in as many years. The successful Armenian offensive in Azerbaijan proper in the summer of 1993 pushed the total of refugee and internally displaced Azeris to — officially — 1.2 million. With nationalist temper running high, talk of peace has brought down successive governments in the same way as reputed oil deals of which Moscow is not a beneficiary. There is a lot of oil mixed with all this blood and misery.

Unofficially, but on the best authority, there are probably around 500,000 refugees. Not in conventional camps, only the Turks, Iranians and Saudis run these. In the main they were absorbed into the general level of misery, further increasing the burden on a society already near breaking point. Sixty per cent of the population live below the breadline and the social safety net is disappearing fast. The IMF arrived in town the day we docked. It demands that the books be balanced, social security cut and bread subsidies removed. Otherwise, it is said, Baku will not get the US$2.4 billion it needs for its stake in the latest oil deal with the West.

The average monthly wage is 14,000 manat — a bus driver earns 6-7,000M — many state employees have not seen a wage packet for months and the minimum cost of a month's basic food is around 20,000M. Easy to see why the arrival of extra mouths to feed has put the mass of the population in a precarious position. Winter is coming and the dying will begin.

Wednesday
Still looking for refugees and out with a European charity delivering flour to state institutions the government has abandoned. An orphanage, a school for abandoned, homeless children, a home for handicapped adults, another school-cum-orphanage, a home for old

people. But they don't want flour — bread is the last remaining cheap item. They want clothes for the children, medicines, paper, pencils, books, blankets.

'We keep making lists,' says the headmaster of a children's home. The children are bright and noisy; the classrooms busy and decorated with pictures of martyrs of the national war. The headmaster plays the accordion and the children sing patriotic songs about the war, the army, freedom and the beloved fatherland. We dance. There are as many blond, obviously Russians as dark little Azeris. 'Many Russians left after independence and the war. They did not always take the children. Grandmothers cannot cope any more, families cannot feed and look after their old folk any more, the state does not look after us anymore.'

The government has said it will repay aid later. When the oil comes in, I suppose. But what are we doing feeding a population its government has subjected to a policy of social triage while it fights a war it cannot win, feuds among itself and cuts deals with the IMF on the back of a population already half starving. And sits on a fortune it cannot turn to account until it ends the war and resolves its internal battles. The human misery is all too evident; as is the lure of oil and gas reserves in excess of the whole of the Gulf, a potentially lucrative market and a strategic position that holds the Muslim states of Central Asia at bay. This town excites the interests of the USA, Turkey, Iran and the EU just as it continues to figure in the larger designs of Moscow that wants its troops back in Azerbaijan as well as Georgia and Armenia.

Conclude there is a lot of oil and politicking mixed up with this aid.

Thursday
'Contract of the century' read the headline in *Moscow News* on 29 September, three days before the coup. 'Azerbaijan and an international consortium of eight major oil companies have agreed to develop three large oil fields on the Caspian Sea shelf... Moscow views the news negatively.'

Four days later, the Russian ambassador in Baku denies that Russia had either instigated the coup or felt any concern over the oil deal.

Now the new rush is on. Walking home in the dark, I was accosted by a man lurking round the long distance bus depot. In broad Lancashire English, he asked me if I knew how the buses worked and if there was one that would get him out of town and into Georgia from whence he could get a flight back to Odessa. A freebooter from Oldham in the hotel business, he saw a bright future: foreign oil men would always need hotel beds and 'I never worry about a bit of a war.'

The government, too, is pinning its hopes and survival on the oil. Meanwhile the economy's a mess, inflation is galloping away, much of the foreign investment that did venture to Baku has packed up and gone home. Meanwhile, the government prints billions of currency notes in Germany to keep going. Unfortunately, I'm told, it never reaches the banks and the whole exercise is repeated more and more frequently.

Friday

The Good, the Bad and the Ugly is showing on AZTV at breakfast time. The news has gone back to its normal, Soviet-style tedium of presidential doings and loyal demonstrations. The only private TV station, financed by local businessmen, was quickly taken over by the government who filled it with a diet of US Westerns and Soviet war films. Suitable fare for a wild frontier seeking to create heroes for its war.

With the exception of a single radio station broadcasting news in Azeri, Russian and English the broadcast media is entirely in the hands of the state. Radio is dull and amateur; TV, says an informant, 'does nothing to meet the national sensibility or the broader needs of the people'. The opposition, naturally, doesn't get a look in.

It turns out that the bulk of the 'press' is local in the extreme. Paper prices and the return of old-style censorship ensure that the 'national' press appears sporadically and is economical with its pages.

The most interesting publication is probably *Azadliq,* close to the opposition Popular Front. It had just re-emerged after three weeks off the market 'because of paper shortages' but there were blank spaces on the front page where copy had been cut, and savage cartoons on censorship.

The media in no way reflects the complex strands that make up the political web of the country. At a distance, Azeri politics looks labyrinthine; closer up it's amazingly simple. It goes something like this. The opposition, mostly grouped under the umbrella of convenience formed in 1989 by the Popular Front, has cornered the market in the high sounding buzz-words: — democracy, free expression, ecology, human rights. Unfortunately it didn't perfom well during its brief tenure of power under its leader President Abulfaz Elchibey, a former dissident of impeccable personal reputation though with some odd views on pan-

148   INDEX ON CENSORSHIP 2 1995

Turkic solidarity and the prospect of a 'national war of reunification' in which Azerbaijan would invade Iran to liberate the 'other half' of the Azeri nation trapped in the land of the mullahs.

He was, however, no match for his wily ex-Politburo rival and present incumbent, President Haidar Aliev. He was manoeuvred out of power within the year, not before he too had stooped to some of the more repressive measures of his successors. The Committee for the Defence of Human Rights and the Committee for Free Speech and the Rights of Journalists are both in the hands of a splinter opposition party. There are now 42 opposition parties. None of them has a popular base and all, like the government itself, are based on clan and regional interests rather than solid policy or principle. Since the loss of its leader and its mauling by Aliev when he came to power in 1993, the PF has kept its head down.

But there is a second, more active opposition front: within the ruling elite represented by Aliev's New Azerbaijan Party. It is they who make the coups, raise their private armies against the government and put regional and clan interests high above those of the state. Prime Minister Suret Husseinov, accused by the president of organising the coup and sacked a few days ago, had already held Elchibey's government to ransom from his base in Gyandzha, 190 miles west of Baku last year, and now defies Aliev by remaining in the city in full view. About the same time in 1993, a former PF leader declared the 'Independent Republic of Lenkoran' on the coast south of Baku. Should Aliev fall, he and his Nakichevan clan could do much the same in their western stronghold.

And all have their foreign masters ready to help them to power and secure their own interests in the process.

It is a fissiparous place, closer to civil war than democracy. Democrats are just as likely as former Communists to carve it up between them. My journalist informant, a professor of history in the university as well as a correspondent for *Moscow Times* and the editor of a local paper, was not sanguine. He was closely linked with one of the newer democratic parties but came out with the familiar platitudes of 'new democrats' everywhere. 'The people are not ready for democracy: like a child with a new computer, they will break it. We only understand dictatorship and we shall have no democracy without dictatorship first.' He ended with a history lesson: 'History gave us two chances at democracy, 1918-1920 and 1992-1993. We made a mess of what little independence we had. All we can do now is put down the roots for the third shot, say in 2010.' ❑

On the streets
of Baku

Street trade: food is still abundant for those who can afford to buy it: most can't

Russian World War II veteran: 'too old to leave, too poor to live'

Left: Street style: 30, maybe 50 per cent unemployment and hustling starts young
Above: The new cemetery for war marytrs, Baku: grave to a 'National Hero of Azerbaijan'

HUMAN RIGHTS

AMNESTY INTERNATIONAL
ARTICLE 19
HUMAN RIGHTS WATCH/ASIA

Shut down

Suharto's open society was short-lived: those who took him at his word paid the price

In his 1990 Independence Day address, President Suharto, in office since 1967, appeared to acknowledge that greater political freedom was essential for a 'dynamic, developing society'. Since then, his New Order government has been officially committed to a policy of openness — *keterbutaan*. Despite scepticism from most intellectuals, activists and journalists, all painfully aware of the government's appalling human rights record since its bloody genesis in the 1965 coup, Suharto was taken at his word. Within months, Indonesia's press was rivalling its freer counterparts in other parts of Asia, peaceful protest was less threatened by the brutality of the state's plethora of security forces, and non-governmental organisations (NGOs) grew in numbers and visibility.

Then, in June 1994, the sham of *keterbutaan* was exposed: three popular weeklies, *Tempo*, *Editor* and *DeTik*, were banned for reporting the financially dubious purchase of old East German warships by Suharto acolyte, technology minister Rudy Habibie. The blatant censorship focused the world's attention on the systematic abuse of rights still unaffected by *keterbutaan*. Article 19's *The Press under Siege* details press closures, Amnesty International's *Power and Impunity: Human Rights under the New Order* gives a comprehensive overview of rights abuses over the past five years, while Human Rights Watch/Asia's *The Limits of Openness* concentrates on seven specific cases during 1993-4. All three reveal the endemic culture of control and repression that continues to sustain the Suharto regime.

The New Order government retains its power with a combination of strict ideological and legal control implemented by force. At the heart of its ideology are the authoritarian 1945 Constitution and *pancasilla*, the five 'guiding principles of the nation', established by President Sukarno, the country's first post-independence leader. Although the principles are characterised by a concern for democracy, humanitarianism and social justice, in practice these are sacrificed to the regime's overriding concern with national unity. Any deviation is dealt with severely. Writers who challenge the state's version of recent history, activists criticising government development plans, squatters whose very presence creates 'disorder', all risk accusations of subversion, treason or Communism. Hundreds of thousands of political opponents have been imprisoned under the Anti-Subversion Law, invoked to repress anti-*pancasilla* elements. In addition, the *Haatzaai Artikelen* (Hate-sowing articles), a legacy from Dutch colonial rule, forbid 'spreading hatred' against the government, an offence punishable by up to seven years' imprisonment.

Power and Impunity points out that, despite recent superficial openness, Indonesian state policy is still dominated by the 'security approach' that originated with the army's ruthless extermination of the Indonesian Communist Party after Suharto's 1965 coup. It relies on a raft of repressive legislation strengthened over the years. The military presence permeates every facet of national life down to village level; force, torture, intimidation and intensive surveillance are the standard means of controlling dissent. Although local commanders purportedly work with the civilian bureaucracy, in practice their word is law and army personnel act with impunity. Mild disciplinary measures against their oppressors are the most that grieving families can expect from the authorities when the security forces are implicated in violent crimes.

Such leniency is not afforded to suspects who do not wear army uniforms. Between 1983 and 1986, some 5,000 alleged criminals were summarily executed by government death squads, their corpses often left to rot in public. Suharto himself has admitted that the killings were officially sanctioned: 'Those who tried to resist had to be shot...corpses were left (in public places)...for the purposes of shock therapy.' According to the country's leading human rights organisation, the Legal Aid Institute, such killings continue: 134 suspected criminals were killed between 1992 and 1994 in Jakarta alone. Fears of increased extrajudicial killings rose with the launching in April 1994 of *Operasi Bersih* (Operation Clean-Up). This joint army-police force was given the task of 'cleansing' Jakarta of criminal elements before the Asia Pacific Economic Co-operation (APEC) summit in November.

One of the positive results of *keterbutaan* was the growing strength of Indonesia's NGOs. However, both *Power and Impunity* and *The Limits of Openness* report the looming presence of a draft presidential decree, which would impose stricter registration procedures and enable the state to dissolve troublesome NGOs acting against the 'national interest'.

Restrictions on the right of association have mainly been used against the country's volatile workforce. Over the last three years, labour unrest has grown. The government has reacted with a mixture of concili-

> **The military presence permeates every facet of life: force, torture and intimidation are the standard means of controlling dissent**

RON GILING/PANOS

On the streets of Jakarta: last call for **Tempo**

ation and repression, responding favourably to calls for an increase in the minimum wage but refusing to sanction the formation of an autonomous trade union. In April 1992, rejecting the government-dominated All Indonesian Workers Union (SPSI), a group of pro-democracy activists and workers founded the independent Indonesian Prosperous Workers Union (SBSI). By January 1994, it claimed nation-wide membership and was actively campaigning for improved conditions. In April, after a series of SBSI rallies degenerated into violence in Medan, North Sumatra, the government arrested hundreds of workers and imprisoned the union's leadership. *The Limits of Openness* presents convincing evidence that military *agents provocateurs* incited the riots.

The regime's reaction to the SBSI was the first indication that the government was rethinking *keterbutaan*; three months later the policy was dead. With the banning of *DeTik*, *Editor* and *Tempo*, the government could no longer pretend that political tolerance and plurality were still its goals.

In the wake of the closures, 58 journalists set up the Alliance of Independent Journalists (AJI). Like the SBSI, the fledgling union failed to gain legal recognition: information minister Haji Harmoko declared the AJI 'unnecessary'. But despite the official Indonesian Press Association's support of the bans and its pursuit of 'unsound' reporters, the AJI continues to fight for press freedom and publishes an underground newspaper, *Indepen*, now believed to have a circulation of 10,000.

During *keterbutaan*, with the press relatively free to perform its role, the world and Indonesians themselves were better informed about Jakarta's continued occupation of East Timor. Forcibly 'integrated' into Indonesia in 1975, Indonesian brutality in the territory continued throughout 1994. Although there were grounds for believing that Suharto was seeking a political settlement to the conflict, the level of unrest has escalated dramatically and is met with increasing intimidation and terror. Groups of hooded men known as 'Ninja Gangs' have appeared in the capital Dili, targeting those suspected of harbouring pro-independence views.

All three reports reserve some of their fire for the indifference of the West: for Australia that viewed the press bannings as an 'internal affair', Britain that continues to be a major arms supplier to Jakarta, and the Clinton administration that insisted the APEC summit was 'not the proper arena' in which to discuss Indonesia's human rights record. ❏
Atanu Roy

Power and Impunity: Human Rights Under the New Order (Amnesty International, 1994, 126pp), available from AI, 1 Easton Street, London WC1X 8DJ; *The Press under Siege: Censorship in Indonesia* (Article 19, November 1994, 31pp), available from A19, 33 Islington High Street, London N1 9LH; *The Limits of Openness* (Human Rights Watch/Asia, September 1994, 145pp), available from HRW, 485 Fifth Avenue, New York, NY 10017-6104

B'TSELEM

Death, lies and videotape

Nidal Tamimi, a 23-year-old Palestinian, was shot dead by soldiers of the Israeli Defence Forces at a checkpoint in the West Bank town of Hebron on 22 October 1994. According to Israeli sources, Nidal Tamimi was shot while trying to stab a soldier. Eyewitnesses, however, say he was unarmed, that he was shot while on the ground, that a knife had been placed next to his body as he lay dead.

The killing of Palestinian civilians in the Occupied Territories by Israeli soldiers is not unusual. What gives the death of Nidal Tamini particular significance is that the whole episode was captured on videotape. It provided conclusive evidence that allegations, always denied, of summary execution by the IDF, do occur. Even so, it took the outrage of the foreign media, persuaded by the tape to report what has become a commonplace in the Occupied Territories, to persuade the Israeli government to open an inquiry. Bassem Eïd, a fieldworker for the Israeli human rights organisation, B'Tselem, tells the story of the investigation that unearthed the evidence.

'The day after Nidal Sa'id Byud a-Tamimi was killed, I went to Hebron to obtain statements from eyewitnesses. There are several shops near the checkpoint, and I entered one of them, a small grocery store. The owner, Muhammed Shafiq Sadr, made this statement about events of the previous day: "I heard shouts and screams 'Allahu Akbar, Allahu Akbar'. I immediately went outside, where I saw a young man in a white shirt and dark trousers clutching a soldier by the throat. The soldier shouted, and the young man called out: 'Allahu Akbar'. Both of them fell to the ground. A soldier standing alongside them tried to free the soldier. Two other soldiers stood about 10 metres away. As I came out from my store, they approached their fallen friend and also tried to free him. After about five minutes, the soldiers succeeded in freeing their colleague and he got up. The four soldiers stepped back about one metre and opened fire on the young man, who had remained lying on the ground. Lots of shots were fired at the young man's chest and head, and he stayed on the ground seriously wounded.

"Youngsters gathered and started to throw stones at the four soldiers. They responded with tear gas, but they also fired several shots of live ammunition into the air. While stones were being thrown at the soldiers, the soldier who had struggled with the Palestinian at the beginning of the incident shot him repeatedly while he was lying in his blood, dead."

'The entire incident, from the time the stone-throwing began, was videotaped by a local journalist, Mazen Daa'na. The tape clearly shows that the soldier shot the Palestinian while he was lying prone and lifeless on the ground.

'I had heard about the killings of Palestinians and the shooting of life-less Palestinian bodies during my work for B'Tselem but had never been able to get conclusive proof. B'Tselem also has statements from IDF soldiers. In one such statement, a reserve soldier indicated that: "In certain cases, during a chase and when life is endangered, the procedure for 'ensuring death' is executed. If we have shot someone and he is lying down, we come within close range, one or two metres, and execute the procedure." What is ensuring death? "We shoot him in the head."

'The evidence of the video gave us the proof we needed. Nevertheless, in a hastily-issued statement, an IDF spokesman claimed that Nidal Tamimi had been shot while trying to stab a soldier.

'B'Tselem wrote to the IDF about the Tamimi case requesting an investigation into allegations that the Palestinian had been shot after he was already dead. In his letter to B'Tselem of 27 November 1994, the chief military prosecutor, Colonel Danny Bari, wrote: "The procedure you call 'ensuring death' does not exist in the IDF. The directives given to soldiers about opening fire are clear..." The directives, we are told, are drafted in conformity with the law. But what about the soldier who appears on the video administering the final *coup de grace* to the prostrate Palestinian? Did he comply with the directives? Will he ever be brought to trial?

'Reports of this incident in the international media created outrage worldwide and compelled the IDF to initiate an inquiry. Such inquiries usually take years to complete, and in most instances the primary issues are ignored or the file is closed on the grounds of insufficient evidence. We have the evidence of the tape. How much longer shall we need to rely on the foreign media to force the IDF to open inquiries into events in the Occupied Territories?' ❑

Bassem Eïd

HUMAN RIGHTS WATCH/ MIDDLE EAST

Who shoots first

The Egyptian government has gone on the offensive against Islamic militants: government troops shoot to kill in the alleys of Cairo and no-one asks questions

President Hosni Mubarak of Egypt is used to the role of statesman and international peace-maker, and he played it well at the Cairo summit in February. But the performance fails to disguise the increasingly tyrannical face of his government in the war raging at home. For three years now after a series of attacks by Islamic militants, tourists have abandoned this land of ancient culture, pyramids and Pharaohs, trekking to calmer beaches. The government has consequently put its foot down, trying to force an end to the violence that is ruining its US$2 billion-a-year tourist industry.

In *Hostage-taking and the Intimidation by the Security Forces*, compiled after spending three years documenting the government's reprisals,

Human Rights Watch/Middle East argues that 'human rights abuses by one party in a situation of internal strife never justify violations by another party.' It continues, 'arbitrary and punitive detention of family members in diverse locations [ie hostage taking] indicate that the practice has become systematic and therefore undoubtedly is sanctioned, if not ordered, at high level within Egypt's security apparatus.'

The first hangings of individuals who had committed, or were sus-

Cairo 1994: waiting for the tourists

DOMINIC DIBBS/PANOS

pected of committing, violent crime began in 1981 after the assassination by Islamic radicals of the then president, Anwar Sadat. At first an average of 10 people were executed every year, but by the end of the 1980s the number of people sentenced to death had increased significantly, whether or not their guilt had been firmly established. The latest figures available from Amnesty International put death sentences for 1994 at 39 and executions at 31.

But for each militant or suspected militant executed, more than 10 new members are recruited into the fold. The government creates martyrs who in turn give birth to others prepared to kill and be killed in the name of the cause. While the report makes no detailed analysis of the extrajudicial mass hangings of Islamic militants, a practice that has been carried out on a large scale over the last 12 months, it confirms the rumours and convincingly demonstrates that the practice has failed to discourage further militant attacks.

As has the deliberate targeting of civilians by the Egyptian security forces, and in particular by State Security Investigation (SSI). In February last year, the Ministry of the Interior initiated a 'shoot to kill' policy in response, it said, to heavy losses in battle with armed militants.

Journalists investigating such deaths express frustration at the reluctance of family members to come forward after relatives have been killed by security forces. One journalist told HRW: 'I've tried to work on this topic [extrajudicial exe-

cutions], but I am confronted with problems. There are no eyewitnesses, and even the families will not testify. The official investigations [by local prosecutors] have nothing in them that can incriminate the police.'

According to the Egyptian Organisation for Human Rights (EOHR), the SSI target anyone acquainted with a suspect. Reports of mass arrests, torture, the detention of women and children, fathers, brothers, and wives threatened with rape, are widespread and thoroughly documented in the HRW report. A peasant in Upper Egypt whose son was killed in custody last July told HRW: 'If I talk to you, can you protect me from the security forces?'

Interior Minister Hassan al-Alfi denies that 'hostage taking' occurs. Al-Alfi has accused Human Rights Watch of showing more concern 'for the rights of the accused than for the rights of the innocent police and civilian victims' of violence. 'Egyptian security forces stick to the law in their confrontation with terrorist elements and do not engage in random arrests as the report says,' al-Alfi told a meeting at a Cairo police officers' club on 31 January. However, the few who have dared to speak out tell a different tale. ❏
Martin Tystad

Human Rights Abuses in Egypt: Hostage-taking and Intimidation by the Security Forces (Human Rights Watch/Middle East, January 1995, 43pp), available from HRW, 485 Fifth Avenue, New York, NY 10017-6104

LEGAL: DEATH PENALTY

A legal column dedicated to the memory of Bernie Simons (1941-1993), radical lawyer and defender of human rights

SAUL LEHRFREUND

Still waiting for justice — Clifton Wright

The number of prisoners on death row in the Caribbean who are innocent victims of miscarriages of justice or who have not had proper legal representation is unknown. But if Clifton Wright's case is anything to go by, many innocent men may be facing execution

Clifton Wright is one of hundreds of prisoners awaiting execution in the Commonwealth Caribbean. His case typifies the use of the death penalty in Jamaica, but common themes are found throughout the English-speaking Caribbean where capital punishment is the mandatory sentence for murder.

Proponents of capital punishment regard the death penalty as a necessary and justifiable sentence within the criminal justice system. Clifton Wright's case brings poverty, politics and a clear denial of justice within

that same system.

Clifton Wright was arrested on 29 August 1981 and has been in custody ever since. On 29 March 1983, he was tried and convicted of murder and sentenced to death. He has now been on death row at St Catherine District Prison, Jamaica, for nearly 12 years.

In 1988, the Inter-American Commission of Human Rights (IACHR) held that he should be released. In July 1992, the Human Rights Committee of the United Nations (UNHRC) made the same recommendations. In February 1994 a petition asking for a full and unconditional pardon, prepared by attorney Jack Hines, acting on behalf of the Jamaica Council for Human Rights (JCHR), was received by the governor-general of Jamaica. The grounds of the petition were based on undisputed evidence presented by the prosecution. It showed that Clifton Wright could not have committed the crime for which he was convicted: he was in police custody when the murder for which he was charged took place.

At his trial in 1983, the government pathologist testifying for the prosecution, Dr Lawrence Richards,

LEGAL

estimated that death had taken place at 2pm on 30 August 1981. But Clifton Wright was taken into custody on 29 August 1981 at approximately 6pm. He had been seen driving a car that belonged to Louis McDonald; the deceased. Mr McDonald had been reported missing and his car reported stolen. The arresting officer searched Wright and his companion, Phillips, and took from them jewellery which was later identified as belonging to the missing man. The police had the body of the victim and had seen two men driving his car which had been stolen. Wright and Phillips were charged with the murder. Phillips was released when the Crown's chief witness failed to identify him, but Wright was convicted and sentenced to death. Even without asking who actually killed McDonald or looking into the police investigation and the conduct of the trial, there can be no doubt that the pathologist's evidence provides Clifton Wright with a cast-iron alibi.

This evidence that was so favourable to Wright was missed both at his first trial and at his subsequent appeal. Inevitably, like the vast majority of those on death row in Jamaica, he was legally aided under the hopelessly inadequate legal aid system. For conducting the defence of a murder trial, a lawyer is paid the fee of JA$175 (cUS$10). On the subject of inadequate legal representation, Florizelle O'Connor, co-ordinator of the JCHR, has said: 'At the stated fees, the legal aid programme provides at best a clear state-

ment for those whom it is designed to serve, that their rights to life and liberty, through adequate legal representation, is not a priority for governments'.

The fact that the crucial evidence was overlooked at his trial meant that Wright's lawyers could not make a submission of no case to answer on the basis that he could not have committed the offence since at the time of the murder he was in police custody.

This evidence was also overlooked by the judge who made no mention of it to the jury and failed, therefore, to direct them to return a verdict of not guilty. The point was also missed on appeal, and the appeal, accordingly, turned down.

The next step in the judicial process was to petition the Judicial Committee of the Privy Council (JCPC) in London. Despite the fact that Jamaica became an independent nation state in 1962, the Privy Council remains its final Appeal Court. It is one of 16 Commonwealth countries retaining the right of appeal to the Judicial Committee, a panel comprised mainly of Law Lords from the House of Lords.

Alan Green, an English barrister, was instructed by Wright's solicitors in London, Messrs Simons Muirhead & Burton, to prepare an application to the JCPC. He discovered Dr Richards' evidence and this was put before the Judicial Committee at a hearing in October 1987. However, in accordance with the view that its jurisdiction does not extend to re-trying a criminal case, the application

The quality of mercy

Founded at the time of the Norman Conquest in the eleventh century, the Judicial Committee of the Privy Council was, at the height of the British Empire, the most powerful appeal court in the world: the last resort for 450 million people. Today, the committee retains jurisdiction over 16 Commonwealth countries who have voluntarily accepted its jurisdiction, and 17 territories and dependencies. The former include New Zealand, Hong Kong and the English-speaking Caribbean.

The committee usually consists of five Law Lords sitting in a court in Downing Street. In cases thought to be particularly important — as in the appeal by Earl Pratt and Ivan Morgan in November 1993 — the number may increase to seven. Pratt and Morgan had been on death row in Jamaica for 14 years; the committee held that to execute a prisoner after long delays was to subject them to inhuman and degrading punishment.

Despite the anachronism of the system and its distant seat in London, it can be argued that the value of the court of the Privy Council lies neither in its historical nor geographical context but in the quality of its justice. Distance strengthens independence and objectivity and reduces the danger of intimidation and corruption. *SL*

Ivan Morgan   Earl Pratt

was dismissed because the Judicial Committee does not entertain points that were not raised either at the trial or on appeal. It stated that it was inappropriate for the obvious inconsistency in the evidence to be raised before it for the first time. In 1987, the JCPC were anxious not to appear as a colonial relic interfering in domestic affairs of Commonwealth countries and adopted a very limited approach to Commonwealth death penalty appeals. Today, the JCPC is not as restrictive and is also concerned not to condone human rights violations or breaches of fundamental rights guaranteed under the constitutions of the countries over whom it has jurisdiction.

By the time the Privy Council dismissed his petition in 1987, Clifton Wright had already been detained in police custody since 29 August 1981. Since his conviction, he has been incarcerated in the appalling conditions of death row at St Catherine District Prison in Kingston, home to all Jamaica's death row inmates. The horrendous physical conditions, alleged beatings, reports of torture and killing and widespread mental illness have been repeatedly documented by Amnesty International and Human Rights Watch/Americas.

Jamaica, Trinidad & Tobago and a number of other Commonwealth Caribbean countries are parties to the American Convention on Human Rights (ACHR) and the International Covenant on Civil and Political

Rural Jamaica: poverty, politics and the denial of justice

Rights (ICCPR). The Inter-American Commission and the Human Rights Committee of the United Nations, both received applications submitted on behalf of Clifton Wright, alleging that his fundamental rights had been violated by the state. On 14 September 1988 the Inter-American Commission stated: 'That since the conviction and sentence are undermined by the record in this case, that the appeals process did not permit for correction, the government of Jamaica has violated the petitioner's fundamental rights.'

It ruled that Clifton Wright should be released.

One of Clifton Wright's letters to the IACHR is of particular interest. 'At the police station no statement was taken from me. The court-appointed attorney came to see me only a few weeks before the trial. At the trial I was not given the opportunity to state whom I got the car from. The trial judge stopped me in the middle of my statement, saying it was not necessary to go further. Had I known it to be a stolen vehicle I would not have driven it, and furthermore, I do not even know why the owner of the car was killed, much less to be involved. Yet I am here in the eyes of society as a killer'.

In January 1989, a further communication was submitted to the UNHRC alleging that Clifton Wright had not been afforded a fair hearing within the meaning of Article 14(1) of the ICCPR. It was submitted that no trial in which the significance of such crucial evidence was overlooked or ignored could be

deemed to be fair; and that the author had suffered a grave and substantial denial of justice. The Human Rights Committee held by its decision of 27 July 1992 that the trial judge should have brought the evidence of Dr Richards to the attention of the jury, even though it was not mentioned by the barrister who was representing him. 'In all the circumstances, and especially given that the trial of the author was for a capital offence, this submission must, in the Committee's view, be deemed a denial of justice and as such constitutes a violation of Article 14(1) of the Covenant.' They recommended that Clifton Wright should be released.

In spite of this, Jamaica has, to date, consistently failed to follow the decisions of the UNHRC and the IACHR. Clifton Wright remains on death row.

A petition of mercy was his last chance of justice. After 13 years, the governor-general of Jamaica had the opportunity to grant him an unconditional pardon in accordance with section 91 of the country's Constitution. But on 11 October 1994, the JCHR were informed that Mr Wright's petition for mercy had been considered and that the governor-general was unable to recommend his release.

If the state takes upon itself the power of life and death over its own citizens, its own conduct must be above reproach and based on unwavering respect for both the letter and the spirit of both national and international law. ❏

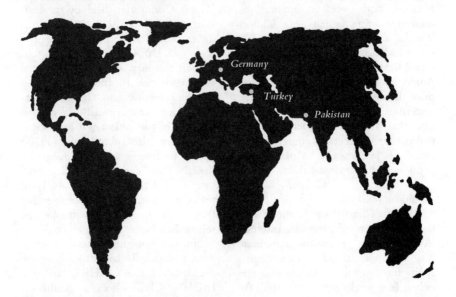

Flashpoint Karachi

In February, the prosecution for blasphemy of two Pakistani Christians — a third had already been murdered before coming to trial — who, it was claimed under oath, had written anti-Islamic graffiti on a wall, defaced the mosque lavatories and thrown blasphemous messages into the mosque, generated huge interest and page-one stories in the western media, hungry, as ever, for evidence of Islamic intolerance. The real importance of the case, however, was not so much the fact of the prosecution as the manner of the acquittal. The chief witness withdrew his evidence claiming his life had been threatened, and the case was thrown out on appeal. The death penalty is mandatory under Pakistan's blasphemy law and, judging by the crowds baying for the life of 14-year-old Salamat Masih and his uncle Rehmat Masih after the acquittal, has huge popular support.

The growing use of the blasphemy laws to silence and intimidate dissent, is not the only way in which the law in Pakistan is being exploited against the people. Impotent in the face of spiralling ethnic and sectarian violence, the government of Benazir Bhutto is turning on opposition MPs. In what Altaf Gauhar, columnist with the English-language daily *The Nation* and the Urdu-language *Nawa-e-Waqt* calls 'a brutal charade of human rights,' it has arrested elected representatives and denied their entry to the National Assembly, abused their fundamental human rights by blatantly fabricating evidence against them, denied fair trials and subverted the judiciary. Those who attempt to oppose the government, particularly its own appointees, know, says Gauhar, 'they will find themselves in preventive custody and, coincidentally, out of a job.'

And finally, to end a dismal month, there was the massacre of Shia worshippers on 25 February. The attack by Sunni gunmen marked a new level in the violence between the sects, not least because the killings took place inside a mosque, an unprecedented act of defilement in the proxy war being financed by Iran and Saudi Arabia.

The funerals that followed degenerated into riots, in the course of which, for reasons not yet clear but 'presumably someone didn't like something we wrote', the Nawa-e-Waqt press building was completely destroyed by a fire bomb. The group, one of Pakistan's biggest press operations, publishes four independent papers and magazines including *The Nation* and *Nawa-e-Waqt*.

In a situation like this, numbers alone say more than any amount of theorising. At the simplest level the facts are these: 800 killed in political violence during 1994 in Karachi alone; 277 killed, again in Karachi, since the start of this year — a figure that has risen by at least two even as this was written.

The European Union's decision in early March to set up a customs union with Turkey is not only an economic but a political coup for Prime Minister Tansu Çiller. The EU made token speeches about human rights and then got things disastrously wrong: instead of making the deal with Turkey contingent on an improvement in its treatment of the Kurds, it watched one of its member states, Germany, close down the Kurdistan Information Bureau in Cologne, and five other Kurdish organisations in Bavaria. ❏

Adam Newey

A censorship chronicle including information from Agence France-Presse (AFP), Amnesty International (AI), Article 19 (A19), the BBC Monitoring Service Summary of World Broadcasts (SWB), the Central American Centre for the Protection of Freedom of Expression (CEPEX), the Committee to Protect Journalists (CPJ), the Canadian Committee to Protect Journalists (CCPJ), the Inter-American Press Association (IAPA), the International Federation of Journalists (IFJ/FIP), the International Federation of Newspaper Publishers (FIEJ), Human Rights Watch (HRW), the Media Institute of Southern Africa (MISA), International PEN (PEN), Open Media Research Institute (OMRI), Reporters Sans Frontières (RSF) and other sources

'Why do we need journalists anyway: the news is the same everyday — "journalist killed", journalist killed"...'

ALBANIA

On 8 February the Supreme Court suspended the prison sentences of four ethnic Greek members of Omonia (*Index* 6/1994) on appeal. A fifth had been released in November. Supreme Court Chief Justice Zef Brozi earlier accused the chief prosecutor's office of trying to prevent him from hearing the appeal, by asking Parliament to lift his immunity from prosecution and allow a criminal investigation against him. (OMRI)

On 11 February 27 MPs, mainly from opposition parties, forced a no-confidence vote against parliamentary president Pjeter Arbnori, accusing him of deliberately breaking parliamentary rules and not making regular reports, as he is obliged to do. (OMRI)

ALGERIA

The Armed Islamic Group (GIA) issued a statement in January threatening all broadcast journalists with death unless they cease their work, concluding: 'Those who fight us with the pen shall be fought with the sword.' (*Al Hayat*, CPJ)

The authorities continue to hamper the press: a ban was imposed on 31 January on the French-language weekly *La Nation* and lifted two days later. On 20 February the weekly *al-Wajh al-Akhar* was again suspended by the interior minister, this time for six months, without any reason being given (*Index* 6/1994).

On 21 February the government's Algerian Press Service news agency withdrew communication links with foreign news services from four publications, *El-Khabar, Le Soir*

d'Algérie, Le Matin and *El-Watan*. (FIEJ, RSF)

The murder of journalists also continues: Abdelhamid Yahiaoui, reporter with the government-owned, Arabic-language, *El Chaab*, was abducted from his Baraki home on 12 January and found the next day with gunshot wounds to the head; Nasser Ouari, who presented an ENTV programme for the hearing-impaired, was killed on 1 February near Algiers; Djamel Ziatar, journalist with daily *Al Djoumhouria*, was killed while visiting his mother's grave in Gdiel, near Oran, on 17 February; and journalist Mohamed Hassaine, formerly with *Alger Républicain*, was found dead after being abducted on 1 March. (RSF, PEN)

Mohammed Zaaf, correspondent for the Italian news agency ANSA, was arrested with his two sons at their home in Algiers on 14 January and accused of 'harbouring a known Islamic militant'. He is believed to have been tortured. (RSF)

A number of well-known figures have been attacked, reportedly by Islamist militants hoping to gain publicity and so circumvent official censorship of their activities. Gunmen shot and wounded film producer Djamel Fezzaz in Algiers on 7 February. Azzedine Medjoubi, the head of the national theatre, was shot dead in Algiers on 13 February. Nabila Djahnine, an architect and leader of a women's organisation, was shot dead in Tizi Ouzou, Kabylie region, on 15 February. Rachid Baba-Ahmed, a rai music producer, was killed in Tlemcen on 16 February. And Abdelhafid Said, a student union leader, was also killed in February. (SWB, AI, *Independent*)

The French-language daily *La Tribune* was suspended until further notice on 5 March, for not respecting an often-ignored provision in the press law, requiring foreign-language publications to also publish an Arabic edition. (RSF)

ANGOLA

Ricardo de Mello (*Index* 3/1994), founding editor of the country's only independent newspaper, *Imparcial Fax*, was gunned down on 18 January outside his home in Luanda. The fatal shooting followed death threats and warnings to stop writing

about military affairs. Eighteen journalists have now been killed since UNITA's rejection of the October 1992 election results. (*Guardian*, MISA)

The independent Angolan Journalists' Union (SJA) reported an attack on 26 January on *Imparcial Fax* reporter Mariano Costa (*Index* 6/1994). *Imparcial Fax* staff claim that one of the cars driven by Costa's assailants was owned by home affairs minister Andre Pitra Petrof. Following further attacks and harassment of workers at the paper, four of its staff applied for visas to enter South Africa. The application was not for political asylum, but for a trip which would allow some respite from the pressure they were under. The South African embassy, however, rejected the application on 15 February on the joint advice of the South African and Angolan Ministries of Home Affairs. (MISA)

ARMENIA

In accordance with a presidential decree of 28 December, several newspapers, including *Yergir*, *Azadamart*, *Arakasd*, *Mounedig*, *Antratarts* and *Nork*, have been closed. The Hailour news agency, the Mikael Varantian printing plant and the Armenian Documentation Centre have also been shut down. The bans, together with the suspension of the Armenian Revolutionary Federation-Dashnaktsutiun (ARF) party, were upheld for six months by the Supreme

Court on 13 January, less than five months before parliamentary elections are due to be held. *Yergir* and *Azadamart* are official ARF publications; the editors of the other publications are ARF members. Many journalists staged demonstrations and sit-ins during January and February to protest the closures. A public announcement on 16 February stated that the publications *Varuzhan*, *Aspar*, *Mtik* and *Mazashkhar* have also been closed. (A19, CCPJ)

AUSTRALIA

On 14 February the Film and Literature Board of Review (FLBR) upheld a decision of the Film Censorship Board (FCB) not to allow the Spanish film *Tras El Cristal* (In a Glass Cage) to be shown at Sydney's Mardi Gras Film Festival. The ruling appears to contradict a 1984 law that frees film festivals from censorship. The FCB found the film incompatible with 'current community standards' owing to scenes of child abuse and the 'implied' murder of young boys. The film tells the story of a sadistic paedophile Nazi doctor and the quest of one of his victims for revenge. (*Australian Financial Review*, Reuter)

BAHRAIN

Three journalists — Ahmed al-Shimlan, Ismat al-Musawi and Ahmed al-Azar — were among more than 1,000 people arrested during further pro-democracy demonstrations on 14 January (*Index* 1/1995). (PEN)

Detained cleric Sheikh Ali Salman (*Index* 1/1995) was deported to Dubai on 15 January, along with two other Shia clerics, Hamza al-Dairi and Haidar al-Sitri. At least 20 other Bahrainis were also deported during January. (*Middle East International*, Committee For The Defence Of Human Rights In Bahrain)

BANGLADESH

Taslima Nasrin's trial on a charge of insulting religious sentiments (*Index* 10/1993, 3/1994, 1/1995) was postponed yet again in January. The next hearing is expected in March. (Reuter, PEN)

In Dhaka on 14 February student members of the fundamentalist Jamaat-e-Islami party attacked and injured Tahmina Shawkat, editor of *Shakuler Khabar*. Three press photographers, Emran Hossain of the *Daily Star,* Asif of *Al-Mujadded*, and Ruhul of *Sangram* were also injured. (RSF)

Moslemuddin Khan, a leader of the opposition Awami League, was shot dead in Khulna on 25 February. The next day, Abul Kalam Azad Chowdhury, a Bangladesh National Party student leader was shot and killed in Khulna, apparently in retaliation. The deaths sparked rioting in which 20 people were injured and the Jamaat-e-Islami offices were burned down. (Reuter)

BELARUS

President Lukasenka denied having introduced censorship

into Belarus at the end of December. On 10 January a group of pro-democracy organisations issued a statement 'on the infringement of the right of Belarusian citizens to free information' and demanded the immediate de-monopolisation of the mass media. On 28 February, addressing state radio and television employees, Lukasenka affirmed the principle of freedom of expression but accused the journalists of 'unwillingness to support the political course of the country's president'. Working for state-owned media, he said, 'obliges you to do everything for the benefit of our state'. (SWB)

BOSNIA-HERCEGOVINA

In early January three journalists with Bosnia-Hercegovina Radio-TV were suspended by the station's new director, Amila Omersoftic, after criticism of their reporting of

Parliament. Omersoftic is said to be a close associate of President Izetbegovic. (Alternative Information Network)

The independent Sarajevo station Radio Zid's deputy director, chief editor, programme editor and entertainment programme director were mobilised into the Bosnian army in January, despite having been granted civilian work permits to ensure that the station stayed on the air. (IFJ, FIEJ)

Bosnian-Serb soldiers kidnapped television journalist Namik Berberovic from a UN armoured car carrying him across ceasefire lines in Sarajevo on 26 January and have refused to allow UN officials visit him in custody. A Spanish and an Italian journalist seized at the same time were released soon after. (Reuter, *Telegraph*)

'Read the Sarajevan press! And its daily supplement'

On 22 February Bosnian-Serb forces detained freelance journalist Shanaat Nahrawand at the same checkpoint from which Namik Berberovic was taken in January. Both she and Berberovic are reported to have been accused of spying. (Reuter, CPJ)

The Bosnian-Serb weekly *Javnost* accused the Serbian government of 'stifling' the journal on 22 February. The 18 February issue did not appear after *Javnost*'s supply of newsprint, which comes from Serbia and is regulated by the government there, failed to materialise. (SWB)

BRAZIL

On 9 December 1994 Wagner dos Santos, a key witness in the case against three military police officers on trial for their part in the 1993 Candelária massacre (*Index* 4&5/1994), was shot and seriously wounded in Rio de Janeiro, despite being under police protection. On 2 February it was reported that dos Santos was unable to leave hospital, owing to fears for his safety. A telephone warning had earlier been received, threatening to kidnap dos Santos from the hospital. Dos Santos claims that the men who shot him were plainclothes police, wanting revenge for his having identified their colleagues. (AI)

Tensions erupted in January between members of the indigenous Macuxi community and the Roraima state military police, following Macuxi protests against a new hydro-

electric dam on the Cotingo River which may affect their land. Plans have so far failed to indicate which areas of land will be flooded by the dam. On 7 January the Roraima state military police expelled some 400 members of the Macuxi community of Caraparu II from their Tamandua livestock-holding area. Since then, military police have set up a blockade to prevent the Macuxi from returning to the area and have told the indians that they will 'use their last bullet' against them if they attempt to return to the area. (AI)

On 12 January *Jornal do Brasil* photographer Alaor Filho was attacked by military security officers while reporting on military exercises in a Rio shanty town. Nelson Carlos, a journalist from the same paper, his driver Carlos Alberto Silva Nascimento, and *O Globo* reporter José Luis Vilhemena were also assaulted as they tried to defend Filho. (IAPA)

BULGARIA

On 15 February the chairman of the Parliamentary Media Committee, George Ganchev, accused foreign media of subjecting Bulgarian media to unfair competition in applications for national airtime and recommended that the official news agency, BTA, be privatised. (SWB)

On 23 February Parliament scrapped the 1992 law preventing former Communists from holding higher academic posts on governing bodies of

universities, research institutes and the Central Examination Board. (OMRI)

CAMBODIA

On 15 February the Information Ministry shut down the paper *Khmer Conscience* for the second time in three months for making allegations of government corruption. On the same day police confiscated part of a special edition of the *Voice of Khmer Youth*, because the paper used the state logo on the cover without permission. Meanwhile the National Assembly's revision of the controversial draft press law (*Index* 1/1995) has substituted the original criminal penalties with civil sanctions. However, vaguely worded offences such as 'degrading' or 'humiliating public authorities' could still lead to punishment of journalists who express anti-government opinions. (Human Rights Task Force)

Chan Rotana, editor of *Voice of Khmer Youth*, was sentenced to one year in prison and fined $2,000 on 27 February for publishing a cartoon and an editorial mocking the country's two prime ministers. Rotana also received a death threat earlier in the month. Second Prime Minister Hun Sen defended the sentence, saying that jailing errant journalists would restore the reputations of senior leaders. (Human Rights Task Force)

CAMEROON

The 13 January edition of the

paper *Le Messager*'s satirical supplement *Le Messager Popoli*, was seized by the authorities (*Index* 1/1995). According to its editor, the supplement was seized because of a picture on its cover representing Chantal Vigouroux, the wife of the head of state. Police also removed the 3 March edition from newsstands in Yaounde and Douala, apparently because of two satirical comic strips it contained. (RSF)

On 1 February William Hallis, a correspondent for the British Broadcasting Corporation (BBC), Vincent T'Sas, correspondent with Reuter, and Charles Yaho, journalist for the weekly *La Nouvelle Expression*, were threatened with tear gas by a group of armed police officers. The journalists were trying to report on an attack by the police on the headquarters of an opposition party. (RSF)

CANADA

Freelance reporter Robert Monastesse was shot in both legs at his home on 20 February. The attack, which police believe was meant as a warning, appears to be linked to Monastesse's recent reports for Montreal's *La Presse* about gang warfare in the city. (CCPJ)

CENTRAL AFRICAN REPUBLIC

The United Nations Human Rights Committee has ruled that the Central African Republic violated five articles of the International Covenant on Civil and Political Rights

by beating and holding a detainee for four years without trial or access to lawyers, medical care or family. After his brother led an unsuccessful coup in 1982, M'Boissona fled to Benin, from where he was forcibly repatriated in 1991. (Interights)

CHINA

It was reported in January that so-called smart-card technology, which would allow satellite television programmes to be vetted before rebroadcasting within China, was offered by Rupert Murdoch in an attempt to persuade Chinese authorities to let him expand his Star TV network there. The system is similar to that used in the West for pay-per-view television. (*Independent*)

Publisher Lu Ping was sentenced to life imprisonment and stripped of political rights for life on 6 January, for illegally publishing 600,000 copies of various books since 1990. An editorial in the *Xinhau Ribao* on 7 January said that 'illegal publishing activities have formed an underground force, disseminating pornography and reactionary books. If we let the situation spread, it will greatly damage the social order.' (SWB)

On 27 January *Xinhau Ribao* reported that, over the previous two months in Jiangsu province alone, almost 2 million illegal publications were seized (of which 676 'posed serious political problems'), 82 printing plants were closed down, 366 unlicensed book

outlets were banned, and 47 'criminals arrested and sentenced'. (SWB)

New secrecy regulations, in force from 1 April, will give customs officials the power to seize any documents, information or materials being sent out of the country, which they suspect could contain state secrets. Any such material will be sent to the appropriate authorities for assessment and, if found not to contain classified information, will be returned to the sender with a clearance certificate. (SWB)

There are grave concerns for the health of writer and reformist political thinker Bao Tong (*Index* 6/1990), who has been in prison since 28 May 1989. Medical experts abroad say Bao's symptoms suggest he could be suffering from cancer. He was sentenced to seven years in prison in 1992. (AI)

Recent publication: *Protestantism in Contemporary China* by Alan Hunter and Chan Kim Kwong (Cambridge University Press, 1995)

COTE D'IVOIRE

Dembélé Fousséni, director of publications, and Kema Brahama, a journalist, both with the monthly *La Plume Libre*, were imprisoned for six months on 2 March for 'disturbing public order, incitement to disorder, and to tribal and religious hatred'. The charges relate to two articles published in the February edition entitled 'The hunt for

Muslim bodies: ethnic purification continues' and 'Ivorian Muslims: the troublesome minority'. (RSF)

On 3 March Abou Cissé, manager, and De Be Kwasi, journalist, with the weekly La Patrie, were imprisoned for one year for 'offences against the head of state'. According to their lawyer the charges were prompted by two articles: one referring to President Bédié's family origins, following the adoption of an electoral code in which only citizens born in the country can stand for the presidency; and the second referring to a financial scandal in 1977, when Bédié was minister of finance. (RSF)

CROATIA

In February the Catholic Church's weekly, Glas Konala, accused unnamed officials of the government and ruling Croatian Democratic Community (HDZ) of trying to use Catholicism as part of a 'state ideology'. (OMRI)

On 2 February MPs launched a Croatian Statehood Campaign aimed at 'nipping in the bud any liberal tendencies'. The campaign accused the media of being anti-Croatian and of falsifying Croatian history. (SWB)

CYPRUS

The trial of the Jehovah's Witness Theocharis Theokli Theocharidis (Index 1/1995), who is refusing to perform military duty on religious grounds, has been postponed

for a fifth time by the Larnaka Military Court, until 31 March. (AI)

CZECH REPUBLIC

On 5 January the Association of Printers (SPP) criticised the trade and industry minister's dismissal of printing company Severografie Usti nad Labem's president Jaromir Lang, who was involved in printing child pornography at his office. The SPP argues his dismissal will force printers to demand the re-establishment of censorship laws, to protect themselves from liability. (Business News)

A draft press law put before the legislature on 7 February would force media organisations to publish government statements in unedited form. It also requires corrections to facts and opinions to be published or broadcast, but contains no freedom of information provision obliging the government to make facts and records available to the public. (Centre for Foreign Journalists, International Press Institute)

ECUADOR

On 7 February José Marino Lanyi and José Llaja Santillan, two Peruvian journalists reporting on the conflict with Peru for Panamerican Television Canal 5, were attacked with tear gas and sticks by around 10 Ecuadorian soldiers who also confiscated equipment and money from them. They were also reportedly forbidden to take Ecuadorian newspapers back to Peru. Jesús Quiroz,

Juan Zacarias, Miguel Silvestre and Jaime Tang, television reporters for Peru's Canal 4, reported receiving anonymous death threats on 8 February and subsequently left the country. (FIP, Instituto Prensa y Sociedad, SWB, PEN)

Theatre director Angel Ulbio Vélez Torres was detained by the army on 7 February near the border with Peru. He is apparently accused of selling a video recording of an Ecuadorian army parade to unknown buyers. (AI)

EGYPT

Workers' Party leader and al-Sha'ab journalist Adel Hussein (Index 1/1995) was released on humanitarian grounds on 18 January. His heart condition reportedly deteriorated while in detention. (PEN)

Film director Youssef Chahine's appeal against the banning of his film al-Muhajer (The Emigrant) (Index 1/1995), was adjourned in February to allow the judges hearing the case to view the film. (Reuter)

Censors removed two stories from February issues of the English-language weekly Middle East Times. One was an interview with lawyer Montasser al-Zayyat (Index 6/1994), and the other a story on the detention of Wafa al Bakri, the widow of lawyer Abdel-Harith Madani who died in detention in 1994. Bakri, apparently arrested because of her testimony in a Human Rights Watch report, has also allegedly been subject to a gagging order. (*Middle East Times*)

Distribution of the *Jerusalem Post* was suspended from 20 February after the foreign minister considered an article by the former Israeli ambassador to the UN, Yehuda Blum, to be offensive. (SWB)

EQUATORIAL GUINEA

Opposition activists Placido Mico, Indalecio Abuy, Indalecio Eko, Tomas Nzo, Amancio Gabriel Nze, José Mecheba Ikaka, and Victorino Bolekia Banay (*Index* 6/1994) were released late in 1994. (AI)

ESTONIA

The country's second-largest Russian-language daily, the state-owned *Estoniya*, was declared bankrupt by the Tallinn City Court on 10 January. Publishing will not be interrupted, however, as the paper is being taken over by the private shareholding company Kronist. (*Baltic Independent*)

ETHIOPIA

Amnesty report journalists Tefera Asmare (*Index* 1&2/1994) and Daniel Kifle (*Index* 4&5/1994) are still serving prison sentences; Girma Endrias, Melaku Tadesse (*Index* 4&5/1994) and Melaku Tsegaye (*Index* 1/1995) have been released. Habtamu Belete, detained for six months, was rearrested on release, but is now thought to have been re-released. Tesfaye Tadesse, Keleme Bogala,

Tewedros Kebede, Kumsa Burayu and Tolera Tessema have been released without charge, and Goshu Moges has been released on appeal against a six-month sentence (*Index* 6/1994). Fourteen journalists were arrested last December: Bekelle Mekonnen and Tesfaye Deressa of the Oromo-language magazine *Urji* have since been released, along with Israel Saboka of *Saifa Nabalaba*; Garoma Bekelle of *Urji* was released on bail in mid-January. Nayk Kassaye is still reported as 'disappeared'. (AI, PEN)

EUROPEAN UNION

The EU decided to maintain Europe's existing non-binding television programming quotas on 9 February, despite pressure from Marcelino Oreja, the culture commissioner, and from France for tighter controls to limit the number of US programmes on European networks. Instead, the use of financial incentives to promote the international competitiveness of European programmes will be investigated. (*Financial Times*)

At a meeting in Brussels on 25 February, the G7 group of industrialised countries decided upon principles for developing the Global Information Infrastructure (GII), or 'information superhighway', focusing on investment and competition. Nine human rights and civil liberties groups expressed concern that the G7 had no plans to adopt a principle promoting the free

exchange of ideas and information when discussing the GII. (OMRI, HRW)

FRANCE

The Paris radio station Radio Skyrock ignored a 24-hour ban on 9 January and instead broadcast a day of listeners' comments on the topic of censorship. The popular station aimed at teenagers was ordered to stop broadcasting after praising the killing of a policeman. The station apologised for the comment but claimed that the ban was excessive. (*International Herald Tribune, Independent*)

GERMANY

The book *Eye For An Eye* by John Sack was withdrawn by the publisher on 17 February, before any copies had been sold. It argues that Stalin deliberately chose Jews to oversee concentration camps in post-war Poland, and has been labelled 'anti-Semitic fodder' by literary critic Eike Geisel. (*International Herald Tribune*)

On 2 March the interior ministry closed down the Kurdistan Information Bureau in Cologne, as well as five other Kurdish organisations in Bavaria. Police raided the groups' offices and confiscated computers, files and books. It had earlier been reported in the Turkish press that the Turkish government had requested Germany to ban local Kurdish groups. (Kurdistan Information Centre)

GHANA

An Accra court has ruled that the controversial Radio Eye case (*Index* 1/1995) be referred to the Supreme Court. Following the ruling, a criminal case against a Radio Eye disc jockey and six directors of the Independent Media Corporation of Ghana (IMCG), which owns the station, was adjourned indefinitely. (*West Africa*, Reuter)

Kwabena Mensah-Bonsu, columnist with the weekly *Free Press*, was jailed for a month on 21 February over an article which accused Supreme Court president, Isaac Kobina Abban, of falsifying court records. The paper's editor, Eben Quarcoo, was fined and imprisoned for one day. (RSF)

GREECE

On 27 January the Greek Foreign Minister Karalos Papoulias refused to attend the commemoration of the liberation of Auschwitz in protest at the Polish government's plan to raise the Macedonian flag during the ceremony. (OMRI)

In late January a court jailed Mehemet Emin Aga for 10 months for assuming the title of Mufti of a northeastern Muslim community. Under a 1990 law, the Greek state has the right to choose the community's two mufti. (Reuter, OMRI)

GUATEMALA

On 4 January Alma Mayán, secretary of the Centro Fray

Bartolomé de las Casas, was attacked by two intruders she discovered searching through documents and files. The centre has operated for two years, providing radio equipment and printing facilities to popular and human rights groups. (AI)

On 28 January a member of the security forces warned Amílcar Méndez Urízar (*Index* 5/1992, 2/1993), president of the indigenous rights group CERJ, of a plot against his life by the head of military intelligence in El Quiché and the local chief of the Treasury Police. (AI)

Alberto Antoniotti Monge, columnist for the daily *El Gráfico*, president of the

Broadcasters' Association, and a former correspondent of Eco, a news programme of the Mexican Televisa chain, was assassinated by five unknown men in Guatemala City on 29 January. (CEPEX)

Human rights activist Senayda Cana Chanay, member of the Mutual Support Group (GAM), was shot and seriously wounded on 6 February as she was leaving her home in the village of Parajo, Buena Esperanza, municipality of San Martín Jilotepeque. The previous day she had reported being followed and questioned by a member of G-2 military intelligence attached to the Chimaltenango military base. (AI)

On 22 February a security guard at the magazine *Tinamit* was murdered. The magazine, which is critical of the government and army, has been a frequent target of gunshots and bomb attacks. (CEPEX)

GUINEA-BISSAU

On 26 January Auzenda Cardoso, assistant manager of the independent weekly *Banobero* and a correspondent for Radio France Internationale, was summoned by the attorney-general in connection with a possible 'abuse of the freedom of the press', following a complaint by a civilian against the reporter. The complaint relates to a report on 15 January about tensions between the president and the prime minister. No reason has been given for the attorney-general's involvement in what is technically a civil matter. (RSF)

The minister of communication, Helder Proenca, suspended the paper *Correio da Guine Bissau* at the end of January, for non-payment of a debt. (RSF)

HAITI

On 23 December 1994 Rotchild François Junior, a journalist with the private radio station Metropole, and Patrick Eliancy, a journalist with the cable channel Télé-Haiti, were attacked and had their equipment damaged by former soldiers who were demonstrating against their discharge from the army. (RSF)

HONG KONG

A Chinese official said on 16 January that some of the 30 human rights and labour organisations in the colony could be classed as 'foreign organisations' and therefore banned under the Basic Law after 1997. (SWB)

INDIA

Gay activists launched a campaign at the beginning of January for the repeal of the law that criminalises homosexual activity (*Index* 1/1995, p199). (*Guardian*)

On 17 January the Supreme Court overruled a threat by the chief election commissioner, TN Seshan, to cancel forthcoming assembly elections in Bihar and Orissa. Seshan had insisted that all voters carry photo-identity cards, but in Bihar only 450,000 cards were issued out of a total electorate of 58 million. The issue of identity cards was part of Seshan's campaign to clean up elections. He has already cut political advertising and candidates' spending. (Reuter)

The following have been detained by the police in Punjab and it is feared they have suffered physical or mental abuse: Harpal Singh Gosal, detained under the Terrorist and Disruptive Activities (Prevention) Act (TADA) on 31 December 1994 and charged on 19 January; Pal Singh, detained on 18 December 1994 and later charged under India's penal code; and Simranjit Singh

Mann, detained on 5 January. (Khalsa Human Rights)

The annual human rights report issued by the US State Department on 1 February accuses Indian security forces of human rights abuses in Kashmir. The report specified extrajudicial executions, torture, kidnapping and the holding of up to 7,000 people without charge in detention centres. An Amnesty International report on Kashmir, issued on 31 January, details 715 cases where Indian security forces are believed to have executed or tortured detainees to death. A report by the International Commission of Jurists (ICJ), issued on 2 March, accuses India of committing between 50 and 350 extrajudicial killings per year in Jammu and Kashmir. (Reuter, AI)

Recent publication: *Torture and Deaths in Custody in Jammu and Kashmir* (AI, January 1995, 125pp)

INDONESIA

Journalists from the banned weekly *Editor* received a licence for a new weekly, *Tiras*, on 9 January (*Index* 4&5/1994). (SWB)

Writer and human rights activist Nuku Soleiman's final appeal against his five-year sentence for 'insulting the president' was rejected by the Supreme Court in mid-January (*Index* 1&2/1994). (PEN)

On 16 January the High Court in Medan increased the

jail sentences of trade union leaders Muchtar Pakaphan (*Index* 6/1994) and Amosi Telumbanua from three to four years and from 15 months to three years respectively. (AI, Reuter)

On 25 January the poet WS Rendra refused to take the stage at a reading in Saparua, West Java, after police forbade him to read four of the twelve poems he was scheduled to read. The Association of Bandung Students, which organised the reading, only received permission to stage the event on condition that the four poems were not read. (Reuter)

On 17 February José Antonio Neves, a Timorese student, was sentenced to four years in prison for 'attacking Indonesian state security'. He was arrested in a post office in May 1994, while attempting to send a fax abroad, containing information about the situation in East Timor. (SWB)

On 1 March the government's Human Rights Commission found that the army had committed human rights abuses during the 12 January Liquica incident in East Timor, when six civilians were killed by troops during a gunfight with separatist guerrillas. (*Singapore Business Times*)

Recent publications: *Deteriorating Human Rights in East Timor* (HRW/Asia, February 1995, 12pp); *The Liquica Killings* (AI, February 1995, 5pp); *Continuing Human Rights Violations* (AI, February 1995, 11pp)

IRAN

Opposition activists Mollah Ahmad Khezri and Majid Sulduzi were abducted at a checkpoint in Iraqi Kurdistan on 26 January by members of the Kurdish Revolutionary Hezbollah, who then handed them over to the Iranian authorities. The two men had fled to Iraqi Kurdistan in 1992 to escape persecution in Iran. (AI)

The government has banned the Tehran-based daily *Jahan-e Islam*, which has not appeared since 8 February. No official charges were brought against the publication, run by hard-line religious critics of the government, but the Ministry of Culture and Islamic Guidance said that these would follow. At the time of the ban, *Jahan-e Islam* was running a series of interviews with Ali Akbar Mohtashemi, a former interior minister and outspoken critic of the government. (CPJ)

On 16 February, shortly after the anniversary of the *fatwa* against British writer Salman Rushdie, a Foreign Ministry spokesman said: 'Muslim nations consider support for the apostate Rushdie as an act of support for slander and an insult against the sacred nations of Islam.' Iran's ambassador to Norway was recalled after hinting that the *fatwa* against Rushdie could be lifted. (SWB)

IRAQ

On 12 January the UN Security Council decided, in a closed session, not to amend the sanctions regime imposed after the invasion of Kuwait in 1990. (*Middle East International*)

Recent publications: *Human Rights Abuses in Iraqi Kurdistan* (AI, February 1995, 141pp); *Iraq and the Rule of Law* (International Commission of Jurists, November 1994)

IRELAND

Television journalist Susan O'Keeffe was acquitted of contempt charges on 27 January (*Index* 4/1993, 6/1995). (National Union of Journalists)

On 1 March the Legislation and Security Committee, established to investigate the events leading up to the fall of the Fianna Fail/Labour coalition government, said that legal constraints had prevented it from issuing conclusions or judgments on the events of last November. The commission reported 'major conflicts of evidence during the inquiry', which it lacked the power to resolve. (*Irish Times*)

On 8 March the Dail passed the abortion information Bill by a majority of 18 votes. President Robinson will refer the matter to the Supreme Court for a test of its constitutionality. The Bill concerns the supply of names and addresses of abortion clinics outside the Republic. This may be judged to be in violation of the Constitution, which acknowledges 'the right to life of the unborn...with due regard to the equal right to life of the mother'. (*Irish Times*)

ISRAEL AND OCCUPIED TERRITORIES

Thirty students were arrested on 27 January after Israeli security forces raided student residences at Al Quds University's College of Science and Technology in Abu Dis, eastern Jerusalem. During the raid five students were injured, materials were confiscated and over 200 students were blindfolded and ordered to sit in a courtyard for seven hours. The students were charged with belonging to Islamist groups. (*Jerusalem Times*, Associated Press)

Travel restrictions on journalists in Israel and the occupied territories (*Index* 6/1994, 1/1995) continue. On 16 February, journalists were barred from covering the Erez checkpoint meeting between PNA chairman Yasser Arafat, Israeli prime minister Yitzhak Rabin and foreign minister Shimon Peres. Access to Jerusalem is open to Israeli and foreign reporters but not to Palestinian journalists from Gaza and the West Bank. (RSF, IFJ)

ITALY

On 17 February the Cabinet approved a draft law to guarantee the equitable use of public and private broadcast media during election campaigns. Among other provisions, party advertisements and opinion polls would be banned 20 days before elections; political advertising which insults opponents or uses deceptive techniques would be banned outright; and a government ombudsman would be given powers to ensure equal airtime for competing parties. (Reuter)

JAPAN

The popular youth magazine *Marco Polo* was closed down by its publishers in January, after it carried an article denying the Holocaust. The article was a rehash of US revisionist tracts, and its publication coincided with the 50th anniversary commemorations of the liberation of Auschwitz. The editor, Kazuyoshi Hanada, offered to print rebuttals in the following issue, but he was sacked and the publication wound up. (Reuter)

JORDAN

Two newspapers, *al-Bilad* and *Hawadeth as-Sa'a*, were suspended by the Ministry of Information in February, for allegedly breaching the publications law. (*Middle East International*)

KENYA

The local government minister, William Ole Ntimama, banned the *Standard* from covering his official functions after it published allegations about his daughter's involvement in irregular land allocations in Nairobi. A journalist from the *Standard*, Kitheka Muno, was charged on 5 January with making 'false and alarming reports' over cattle thefts in December. (*Ngao*)

Three MPs who were due to attend a church service with the families of victims of ethnic violence, were arrested in Longonot on 15 January. Njenja Mungai, MP for Molo, Lawali Oyondi and Francis Wanyange, MPs for the Nakuru area, were arrested with a Ford-Kenya official, Joel Odoyo Ondiala, a councillor, Mwangi Gikonyo, and Mungai's brother, John Njenja Mungai, and charged with promoting 'warlike activities', 'uttering words with seditious intention', and making threats against President Moi's Kalenjin ethnic group. Oyondi, Wanyange, John Mungai and Gikonyo have since been released and the charges against them dropped, but Njenja Mungai is reportedly held under armed guard. The arrests came after attacks by Masai against Kikuyu in January and the forced removal of Kikuyu people from Naivasha to Central Province in December, as part of a drive to secure the Rift Valley for the Kalenjin and the Masai. (*Economist*, AI)

The Centre for Law and Research International was forcibly closed in February after its publication, *Clarion*, carried a report in January accusing the government of involvement in high-level corruption. (*Financial Times*, AFP)

A radical Muslim cleric, Sheikh Balala, has been stripped of his citizenship and passport while in Germany, it was reported in February. Balala is the founder of the

Islamic Party of Kenya, formerly in alliance with Ford-Kenya. (*New African*)

On 16 February PEN called for an independent investigation into an arson attack on *Finance Magazine*. The fire follows the repeated imprisonment of Njehu Gatabaki, editor and owner of the magazine, and intimidation of members of staff. (PEN)

Recent publication: *Attacks on Human Rights through Misuse of Criminal Charges in Kenya, Tanzania, Uganda, Zambia and Zimbabwe* (AI, January 1995, 15pp)

KYRGYZSTAN

President Askar Akayev has called upon the country's journalists to refrain from expressing extreme views and to be balanced in their criticism of the country's leadership. The presidential press service reported on 16 January that Akayev has rejected various proposals for a new law on the media as an attempt to reinstate censorship. (OMRI)

The author Chingiz Aytmatov was elected to Parliament on 5 February, in apparent contravention of the Constitution, which states that all parliamentary candidates must have lived in Kyrgyzstan for five years prior to the election. Aytmatov has been in Luxembourg for the past four years, first as Soviet, and then as Russian ambassador. The Electoral Commission chairman's statement on 8 February that an exception could be made for 'an out-standing author', caused outrage among democrats. (SWB)

LEBANON

Three books by the late liberal Islamic writer al-Sadeq al-Nayhoum were seized by police on 13 January at the request of a leading Sunni Muslim cleric. Lebanese law allows for the confiscation of books considered offensive to religious leaders. In a statement to protest the seizure, 120 Christian and Muslim writers and artists called on the books' publisher, Dar al-Rayyes, to appeal against the law. (Reuter)

MACEDONIA

On 17 February one person was shot dead and 20 were injured after a police crackdown on the illegal Albanian-language university in Tetovo (*Index* 1/1995). The university's rector, Fadil Sulejmani, was arrested. On 23 February Nevzat Halili, leader of the Party for People's Union, and Musli Halimi, a professor at the university, were arrested along with other Albanian activists during a demonstration against the university by Macedonian students. Macedonian law prohibits higher education in Albanian. (OMRI)

In February the Skopje Pedagogical Academy agreed to offer Albanian-language instruction in education, psychology and sociology. Ethnic Albanian students have been boycotting classes at the academy for more than two months to protest the lack of Albanian-language instruction. (OMRI)

MALAYSIA

On 4 February the information minister, Datuk Mohammed, directed the country's three television channels and the Film Censorship Board not to show material containing scenes of sex and violence. He said that stations should not think of revenues alone, but also of their wider social responsibilities. In late January the prime minister complained that broadcasters were continuing to screen 'inappropriate' material 'despite repeated requests to cut such sequences'. There has been a growing campaign against sex and violence on television from Islamic groups. (*Asiaweek, Far Eastern Economic Review*)

On 27 February Lim Kit Siang, leader of the opposition Democratic Action Party (DAP), said that three Chinese-language papers had stopped all reporting on the DAP after the government accused them of 'undermining racial and religious harmony'. Several Chinese papers were previously accused by pro-government parties of supporting the opposition in the 1990 election campaign. The prime minister is expected to call a general election in April. (RSF, Reuter)

Lim Kit Siang's son, a DAP youth leader, pleaded not guilty to sedition on 1 March. The charge arose from allegations of sexual impropriety and conflict of interest Lim the younger made against a federal cabinet minister in a debate on 19 January. He faces a heavy fine or three years in prison if convicted. (Reuter)

MALDIVES

President Gayoom announced on 28 February that he will introduce new laws to fight Muslim religious extremism. The government will not allow extremists to fragment society, he said. The law is believed to be aimed at the Wahabi sect. (Reuter)

Recent publication: *Freedom of Expression Under Threat* (AI, February 1995, 6pp)

MAURITANIA

A number of journalists came under attack from police while covering disturbances in Nouakchott in late January: Abdellah Ould Mohamdi of the Middle East Broadcasting Corporation; Sidi Mohammed Ould Soumbra and Mohammed Ali Ould Abady of *El Mouhit*; journalist Karine Ancellin-Saleck, photographer Baba Fall, and editor Bah Ould Saleck from *Mauritanie Nouvelles*; and Abdellah Ould Hormetellah of *Le Calame*, were all assaulted and had material confiscated. Bah Ould Saleck reported that he was again attacked by police who destroyed his press card on 27 January. (CPJ, RSF, PEN)

An international seminar on the press organised by the Study and Research Group on Democracy and Economic and Social Development (GERDDES), which was due to open on 25 February, was banned by the Interior Ministry on the grounds that the organisers had not obtained official accreditation for the event. (SWB)

MEXICO

Ruperto Armenta Gerardo, editor of the Guasave-based weekly *El Regional* in the state of Sinaloa, was beaten to death by unidentified men on 5 February. (CPJ)

On 7 February civil rights campaigner, journalist and political activist Amado Avendaño Figueroa (*Index* 1&2/1994, 4&5/1994) was falsely accused by the Ministry of Defense of attacking and injuring a soldier in Chiapas. Unfounded criminal accusations by official bodies figure prominently among dozens of reports of harassment, intimidation, threats and attacks against human rights monitors, and civil and political activists in the state. (AI)

On 8 February María Gloria Guevara Niebla was detained in Mexico City and reportedly tortured, threatened with her two-year-old son's torture and death, and forced to sign a confession. She is among at least 13 alleged members of the Zapatista National Liberation Army (EZLN) detained and tortured between 8 and 10 February. The federal Public Security Secretariat announced a new operation on 10 February to protect journalists in the mass media from attack by the EZLN. (AI)

On 10 February the offices of the Co-ordination of Non-Governmental Organisations Working for Peace (CONPAZ) in San Cristóbal de las Casas, Chiapas, were raided by Federal Judicial Police. Members of CONPAZ were reportedly followed by the police when they left their offices prior to the raid. (AI)

CONPAZ reported on 11 February that *Irish Times* journalist Michael McCaughan was among a group of volunteers missing from the Morelia community in Altamirano, Chiapas, following a new Mexican army offensive in the region. (Asociación Pro Derechos Humanos de España)

On 11 Febuary Ramiro Arciniega Martínez, school head teacher and leader of the teachers' union in Tehuacán, state of Puebla, was detained by members of the army and the Federal Judicial Police (PJF), reportedly tortured and forced to confess alleged involvement with the EZLN. (AI)

An Inter-American Press Association (IAPA) mission to investigate the murders of *El Crucero* editor Jorge Martín Dorantes (*Index* 3/1994), journalist Enrique Peralta Torres and *La Unión de Morelos* managing editor José Luis Rojas in mid-1994 (*Index* 4&5/1994) confirmed that there were flaws and contradictions in the official investigations into the killings. (IAPA)

NAMIBIA

Members of the Namibian Media Women's Association (NAMWA) are calling for harsher sentences on rapists after an apparent increase in assaults against women. NAMWA's chair, Leefa Martin, says that she is less likely to get sent out to cover a story than a male colleague, because of her greater vulnerability to attack. (MISA)

Prime Minister Habe Geingob has issued a draft Public Service Bill, which includes measures to prevent civil servants from publicly criticising government policy or disclosing unauthorised information. Freedom of speech and access to information is guaranteed in the Namibian Constitution. (MISA)

NETHERLANDS

The government's appeal against the acquittal of author Graa Boomsma (*Index* 3/1994, 4&5/1994) was dismissed on 26 January. Boomsma reports receiving threatening telephone calls throughout January. (PEN)

NEW ZEALAND

A group of Chinese parents are threatening go to court to block a proposal to bar non-English-speaking children from Auckland schools. The Auckland Primary Principals Association (APPA) made the proposal after Epsom Normal School said that new applicants would have to prove their competency in English. (*International Herald Tribune*)

NIGERIA

On 19 January security agents raided the shared offices of the Campaign for Democracy (CD) alliance and the Committee for the Defence of Human Rights (CDHR). It was the third raid on the offices in one week, following the arrests of CD president Beko Ransome-Kuti and Femi Falana, president of the National Association of Democratic Lawyers on 12 January. (Reuter)

Military authorities in Oyo state have suspended indefinitely the entire staff of a local government-owned radio and television station after they went on strike over pay in early February. The premises of the Broadcasting Corporation of Oyo State (BCOS) have been sealed off by soldiers. (Reuter)

On 7 February General Abacha extended by a further six months the ban on the publications of the independent Guardian newspaper group (*Index* 4&5/1994). (Reuter)

The trial of Ken Saro-Wiwa (*Index* 3/1994, 6/1994, 1/1995) was again postponed until 21 February, to allow him time to consult his lawyers. Saro-Wiwa, detained since May 1994, was formally charged on 6 February with procuring and counselling the murder of four Ogoni people on 21 May 1994. Saro-Wiwa has made many public statements against violence. It is widely believed his trial is politically motivated due to

the international support Saro-Wiwa has mobilised for the Ogoni's cause. When the trial started, military personnel refused to permit journalists from the opposition newspapers *Tell* and *The News* to enter the court. When defence lawyers protested this, they were allegedly roughed up by army officers. (PEN)

PAKISTAN

The Karachi-based Mohajir National Movement (MQM) petitioned the Supreme Court on 17 January over the state's alleged violations of the political and economic rights of the Mohajir community. They claim that the 29-month army occupation of the city was an attempt by the former government to suppress their party, and asked the court to nullify the October 1993 election. (Reuter)

Abdul Ameer, an Iraqi Kurd refugee who went on hunger strike in support of claims for resettlement of Kurdish refugees in Sweden, died in hospital on 18 January. During the 1990-91 Gulf crisis, 1,500 Kurds fled to Pakistan. Four other Kurds on hunger strike claim they are at risk in Pakistan. The UN High Commissioner for Refugees (UNCHR) said it could not resettle them and that they are safe in Pakistan. (Reuter)

Pervaiz Elahi, the opposition leader in the Punjab regional assembly and a supporter of former prime minister Nawaz Sharif, was arrested on 18 January for alleged financial fraud. Elahi denied the charge saying the government is using the courts to intimidate its opponents. (Reuter)

The Human Rights Commission of Pakistan (HRCP) states in its annual report issued on 28 January that Pakistan is failing to tackle widespread human rights abuses. The HRCP says that more than 800 people were killed in political violence during 1994 in the city of Karachi; at least three journalists were killed, more than a dozen harassed and seven newspaper offices attacked; and four journalists of the Ahmadi sect were charged under the blasphemy law, which carries the death penalty. (Reuter)

Two Pakistani Catholics were sentenced to death on 9 February under the penal code of 1992 which makes blasphemy a capital offence. Salamat Masih, 14, and Rehmat Masih, his uncle, were also sentenced to two years' hard labour before their execution. Their appeal was allowed on 24 February, when an important prosecution witness withdrew his evidence, obliging the appeal judges to dismiss the charges. Islamist militants claimed that prime minister Benazir Bhutto had interceded in the case and called for her death in a demonstration at Lahore. (Reuter, *Times*, AI)

Sunni militant gunmen murdered 20 worshippers in attacks on two Shi'ite mosques in Karachi on 25 February. A 15-year-old Sunni boy was shot dead in his shop later the same day, apparently in revenge. 250 people have been killed in ethnic and sectarian attacks in Karachi since 1 January. During the funeral of the victims of the Karachi mosque killings, rioters burned down the offices belonging to the Nawa-e Waqt Press Group. Journalists working for *The Nation*, *Nawa-e-Waqt*, *Family Magazine* and *Phool* were beaten by the mob. The prime minister condemned the attack and promised government protection for newspapers. (Reuter, RSF, Pakistan Press Foundation)

Recent publication: *The Pattern Persists: Torture, Deaths in Custody, Extrajudicial Executions and 'Disappearances' Under the PPP Government* (AI, January 1995, 55pp)

PALESTINE (GAZA-JERICHO)

Palestinian police raided the premises of the weekly *al-Istiqlal* on 6 February and arrested the publisher, Alaa al-Saftawi (*Index* 6/1994), and five journalists, Atiyeh Abu Mansour, Khaled Sadeq, Nahed Kutkut, Muhammed Sayyad and Zakariya Madhun. At least 51 suspected members of the Democratic Front for the Liberation of Palestine and the Islamist groups Hamas and Islamic Jihad have also been held without charge since 6 February. (CPJ, AI)

Raji Sourani, director of the Gaza Centre for Rights and Law, was arrested in the early hours of 15 February by Palestinian police and detained for sixteen hours. He was questioned by attorney-general Khaled Qudra over a statement issued by the Centre criticising the newly appointed military courts. (*Jerusalem Times*, Telegraph)

On 25 February *al-Rased*, the newsletter of the PNA's broadcasting organisation, the Voice of Palestine, was banned for publishing an article criticising King Hussein of Jordan. (CPJ)

Recent publication: *The Gaza Strip and Jericho: Human Rights Under Palestinian Partial Self-Rule* (HRW/Middle East, February 1995, 50pp)

PAPUA NEW GUINEA

Recent publications: *Bougainville: An Agenda for Human Rights* (AI, February 1995, 6pp); *Bougainville: Political Killings and 'Disappearances' Continue* (AI, March 1995, 5pp)

PERU

On 4 January the television station Canal 11 RBC's signal was interrupted and the station forced off the air for four days, following an interview in which General Luis Cisneros Visquerra criticised the government. According to Ricardo Belmont Cassinelli, mayor of Lima and one of the station's owners, there have been 18 such blackouts at the station during the previous three months. Belmont is a presidential candidate in the April elections, and a well-known critic of President

FROM AZADLIQ, AZERBAIJAN

Рас. Р.ШЕРИФ

Fujimori. (Instituto Prensa y Sociedad)

Foreign journalists covering the war with Ecuador have been severely hampered by the authorities. The Association for the Foreign Press in Peru (APEP) reports that two trips organised for foreign press pools were cancelled on 4 and 5 February, and that foreign correspondents were denied access to the conflict area, reporting instead from Peruvian military bases dozens of kilometres away. Local journalists also complained at the end of February that they are routinely denied access to hospitals, army headquarters and airports in the area. (RSF)

On 12 February two Ecuadorian journalists,

Ramiro Ueva and Pablo Reyes, were abducted by Peruvian troops who accused them of being spies and threatened them with execution. (SWB)

POLAND

The Supreme Court ruled on 19 January that journalists must reveal their sources of information, if required by a prosecutor or judge. Journalists who insist on protecting sources can be fined or imprisoned for up to a month. The ruling has been widely criticised in the media. (SWB)

ROMANIA

On 19 January the daily *Ziua* suspended printing for the second time in a month, accusing the sole, state-

owned, paper mill of refusing to deliver newsprint (*Index* 1/1995). (Centre for Foreign Journalists)

On 23 February the government dismissed the Mayor of Brasov, a member of the opposition Democratic Convention, along with mayors, councillors and top officials in 27 other towns. Large numbers of local politicians have been dismissed since 1992, most of them members of opposition parties. (OMRI)

Proposed amendments to the Penal Code, expected to be passed by Parliament in March, would impose long prison terms for offences including 'damaging the reputation of a public official or publishing false information that might damage state security or international relations'. (International Press Institute)

RUSSIAN FEDERATION

Russia: On 22 February Alexei Kostin (*Index* 1&2/1994), founder and publisher of the erotic journal *Yeshcho*, was brought to trial after being detained since February 1994. Under Russian law, the maximum term of detention prior to trial is nine months. The case against Kostin is believed to have been stimulated more by *Yeshcho*'s political content than its contravention of the pornography statutes. On 24 February he was released pending the trial's result. (CPJ, PEN)

Under a proposed new law, which has passed its second

reading in the Duma, the Federal Counter-Intelligence Service (FSK) will be renamed the Federal Security Service (FSS) and granted a wider range of responsibilities, including crime fighting. The bill stipulates that surveillance operations against suspects would no longer be made accountable to the public prosecutor's office. Although intended to combat organised crime, the proposed law has raised fears of a revived KGB. (*Times*)

President Yeltsin signed a decree in January providing for the privatisation of 49 per cent of the television station Ostankino, which is now known as Russian Public Television, with Yeltsin as chairman of its Board of Guardians. It is a public corporation with 51 per cent of the shares held by the state but without state subsidies. (Centre for Foreign Journalists)

The newspaper *Ekspress Khronika* ceased publication on 17 February, owing to a lack of financial support. *Express Khronika* was the successor to the premier samizdat journal of the Soviet era, *Chronicle of Current Events.* (SWB)

The Duma adopted a resolution demanding a bill to outlaw 'fascist propaganda, pageantry, international contacts and paramilitary organisations' on 14 February. (SWB)

On 22 February the Duma overrode a presidential veto of a new law on demonstrations, by which Yeltsin was intending to ban gatherings of people in the immediate vicinity of public buildings. (Interfax)

Vladislav Listyev, 38, presenter of the highly popular news talk show *Peak Hour* and the key figure in the reorganisation of Ostankino, was shot dead while returning to his Moscow apartment late in the evening of 2 March. The murder has been attributed to organised crime, with a range of suggested motives including: the staff reshuffles and redistribution of airtime initiated by Listyev; the decision to ban all advertising on Ostankino; and inside information that Listyev might have had on the proposed sale of shares in Ostankino/Russian Public Television. Despite the extraordinary degree of public outrage at the killing, the media were excluded from Listyev's funeral service, purportedly at the request of his family. However, Interior Ministry officials were present outside the cemetery to prevent journalists from entering. Under the proposed law on demonstrations (see above), political meetings at cemeteries would be banned. (Reuter, SWB)

Chechnya: Russian prime minister Viktor Chernomyrdin urged journalists at the All-Russian State Television and Radio Broadcasting Company to report the events in Chechnya 'without bias' and admitted that there had been 'no proper information measures' to cover the situation there. (SWB)

Russian authorities reportedly refused to allow an Iranian television crew to enter Chechnya on 14 February, despite the team having obtained visas for the visit. (SWB)

Kaliningrad: A new law 'On the Protection of the Russian Federation State in Kaliningrad Region' was proposed in early January. It would forbid the use of German names in streets and other place names in the region. Kaliningrad, formerly east Prussia, has no non-Soviet Russian heritage to revert to. (SWB)

RWANDA

Edouard Mutsinzi, editor of *Le Messager-Intumwa,* is in a coma after an assassination attempt on 29 January. He is well known as a critic of the former government but it is believed that this attack is linked to his criticism of excesses committed by RPF soldiers. (RSF)

Recent publication: *Under the Volcanoes: Rwanda's Refugee Crisis* (International Federation of Red Cross and Red Crescent Societies, January 1995, 39pp)

SAUDI ARABIA

On 20 February Ahmed al-Seweifi, a journalist with the bi-weekly *al-Sha'ab,* was refused entry to the country, despite having been issued with a visa by the Saudi embassy in Cairo. Immigration authorities told him he was on a list of people banned from visiting the country. (RSF)

SERBIA-MONTENEGRO

Serbia: Television stations were asked in January to restrict their hours of broadcasting to between 6.30 pm and 11 pm to save electricity. Power shortages have been common across the region this winter, but opposition parties accuse President Milosevic of exporting energy supplies in exchange for oil. (OMRI)

On 4 February staff at *Nasa Borba*, which was legally registered on 20 January, were prevented from entering the paper's offices on the orders of the state liquidator Radomir Radovic. They were unable to retrieve office equipment belonging to the paper. *Nasa Borba* is now operating from the offices of the trade union Nezavistnost. On 23 February the European Union allocated $120,000 to enable *Nasa Borba* to buy newsprint (*Index* 1/1995). (FIEJ, OMRI)

On 8 February the Belgrade station NTV Studio B was informed that it is not lawfully registered, because the 1991 court decision which made it a joint-stock company has been reversed. Observers fear that the city assembly is attempting a takeover of Belgrade's only independent broadcast medium, using means similar to those used to take over the paper *Borba* in December. In a separate case, the Kragujevac weekly *Svetlost* was also told that it cannot register as a joint-stock company and on 16 February it

was removed from the media register. (FIEJ, OMRI, SWB)

On 16 February Colonel Ljubodrag Stojadinovic was dismissed from his post as head of the General Staff's information bureau for publicly criticising the federal President. He is to be tried by a military court for damaging the army's reputation. (SWB)

On 18 February Serbian authorities imposed a total news blackout on talks between President Slobodan Milosevic and Russian foreign minister Andrei Kozyrev. (OMRI)

Montenegro: On 5 January the opposition station TV Montena was told to cease broadcasting or face criminal prosecution. The Podgorica station Montenegropublic also had its broadcasting permit annulled by the Broadcasting Allocation Committee. (Alternative Information Network)

On 20 January the independent weekly *Monitor* reported that 20 people from Cetinje were imprisoned for slandering Montenegrin President Momir Bulatovic. The entire leadership of the ethnic-Muslim Party of Democratic Action for Montenegro (SDA) has also been imprisoned for 'separatist activity' and MP Acim Visjnic, of the extreme nationalist Serbian Radical Party, was sentenced to five months for 'slandering the Republic and President of Montenegro'. (OMRI)

Kosovo: On 29 January it was reported that about 200 eth-

nic-Albanian former police officers, arrested since November 1994 (*Index* 1/1995), have been tortured and interrogated without lawyers present. (OMRI, AI)

SIERRA LEONE

Siaka Massaquoi, editor of the weekly paper *Vision* and president of the Sierra Leone Association of Journalists, was arrested on 12 January after accusing the country's military rulers of 'celebrating Christmas with pot-smoking musicians' while rebels launched a military offensive. He was released the same day, but has been called in for questioning every day since. (*Guardian*, PEN)

New Breed journalists Julius Spencer, Donald John and Mohammed Bangura, and sales manager Alfred Conteh (*Index* 1/1995), were released on bail in the middle of January. Bangura was released on health grounds, and the case against him will not proceed at present. (PEN)

Chernor-Ojukwu Sesay, Freetown correspondent for the Gambian *Daily Observer*, was detained for 32 hours in January by a team of military and police officers for offences pertaining to 'subversive documents'. Articles and music cassettes were seized from his office. (*Daily Observer*)

SOUTH AFRICA

It was revealed in early January that the former National Party government granted immunity from prosecution to 3,500 police officers just before leaving office. The Cabinet has since invalidated the amnesty because it prejudices the enquiries of the Truth Commission, set up to investigate state-sponsored human rights abuses under apartheid. (*Weekly Mail & Guardian, International Herald Tribune*)

The South African Broadcasting Corporation (SABC) has outlined ambitious plans to establish 11 unilingual national radio stations, and to use all the country's 11 official languages in locally made drama and current affairs programming. (*Weekly Mail & Guardian*)

The recent closure of the independent weekly *South* marks the sixth 'alternative' newspaper to fold within the last year (*Index* 1/1995). (*Southern Africa Report*)

The ANC has responded harshly to newspaper reports that Cyril Ramaphosa intended standing down as party chairman in favour of Thabo Mbeki at this year's party congress. The ANC has called on newspapers to refrain from using 'wild allegations' and 'malicious reporting' of ANC affairs. (MISA)

SLOVAKIA

On 18 February 52 Slovak Radio journalists wrote an open letter to *Sme* to protest the dismissal of the station's Washington correspondent, Peter Suska. The letter, addressed to the new director of Slovak Radio, Jan Tuzinsky, claims the dismissal was motivated by a recent report by Suska criticising a government official. (OMRI)

On 21 February the Cabinet set up a new media council, which will be an advisory organ without decision-making power. The 20-member council includes 15 government members, four from the Association of Slovak Journalists and one from the Slovak Syndicate of Journalists. (OMRI)

It was reported on 23 February that over 100,000 people have signed a petition to protest threats to freedom of speech. The petitioners are particularly concerned about the cancellation of three satirical television programmes, *The Milan Markovic Evening Show* (*Index* 1/1995), *Apropo TV* and *Halusky*. (OMRI)

An unnamed cameraman from the German station ARD in Bratislava was assaulted by Slovak police while trying to film a Greenpeace demonstration against the Mochovce nuclear power station on 30 February. (SWB)

SOMALIA

Marcello Palmisano, a cameraman with the Italian television station TG2, was killed in an ambush by armed men on 9 February. TG2 presenter Carmen Lasorella was wounded in the attack. (SWB)

SRI LANKA

Three commissions of inquiry to investigate murders and disappearances opened on 10 January. Human rights groups say that about 60,000 people, mainly young men, disappeared or were killed between 1988 and 1990, when the UNP government crushed a rebellion. (Reuter)

'Such a pleasure to see you in good health, Eyadema' (Togo)

Prior to the Pope's visit in

January, the Federation of Buddhist Organisations insisted that the Vatican withdraw offensive passages about Buddhism in the Pope's book, *Crossing the Threshold of Hope,* and issue an apology. The Pope describes Buddhism as an atheistic system with a negative doctrine of salvation. On 11 January arsonists attacked a Buddhist shrine one day after a Catholic church was damaged by fire. (Reuter)

Lasantha Wickrematunga, editor of the *Sunday Leader,* and his wife Raine, features editor in the same paper, were attacked by unidentified men in Colombo on 7 February. Wickrematunga is a well-known critic of President Kumaratunga and regularly gives details of her social life in his reports. (Reuter, RSF)

President Kumaratunga said on 9 February that Sri Lanka will formulate a code of ethics to prevent abuses of media freedom. She claimed that the press has 'a wild ass's freedom' and that 'there is utterly irresponsible journalism going on at the moment'. (Reuter)

Over 250 people protested outside the state-owned Sri Lanka Broadcasting Corporation (SLBC) on 10 February against both the axing on 6 February of a current affairs programme that criticised the government and the attack on Lasantha Wickrematunga (above). (Reuters)

Sinha Ratnatunga, editor of the *Sunday Times,* and reporters at *Lakbima* were questioned by police on 22 February about articles in the two papers about President Kumaratunga's extravagant lifestyle. Ratnatunga may face defamation charges. (Reuter)

Recent publication: *Words into Action: Censorship and Media Reform in Sri Lanka* (A19, *Censorship News* issue 39, March 1995, 22pp)

SWAZILAND

The High Court ruled on 24 November 1994 that seven supporters of the opposition People's United Democratic Movement (Pudemo) were guilty of sedition for participating in a peaceful demonstration without proper police permission. (AI)

TAIWAN

On 16 January four unlicensed radio stations in different parts of the island were closed down. Police squads reportedly used helicopters to remove *Voice of Taiwan*'s transmitter mast. On 3 January, approximately 300 police officers raided *TNT Voice of New Formosa.* The raids are the latest in a long series that have shut down several stations over the past 12 months (*Index* 4&5/1994). (CPJ)

TANZANIA

With the first multi-party elections to be held in October 1995, the government is tightening control over the media by establishing an Information Services Department to channel news about the government and prevent direct contact between the press and officials. A controversial bill to licence journalists, which was shelved after protests in 1993, has been revived. It would require journalists to have a university degree, thereby excluding some of Tanzania's leading and most outspoken writers. The government has also taken advantage of a shortage of newsprint to put pressure on the independent press. (MISA, *Family Mirror*)

The editor of *Mwana-Mama,* Godfrey Mhando, five of his staff, and the editor of *Heko*'s (and the alleged financer of *Mwana-Mama*) Ben Mtobwa, have all been charged with publishing pornography after *Mwana-Mama* ran an exposé of Dar es Salaam's illegal but flourishing porn industry. (MISA)

TOGO

The five-year jail term imposed on *Tribune des Démocrates* journalist Martin Gbenouaga (*Index* 3/1994) was reduced on appeal to one year in January. A presidential decree then cancelled the sentence and Gbenouaga was released on 17 January. He had been convicted for writing that President Eyadema and other African leaders held power 'by force of arms, distortions, lies, and tribalism'. (Reuter, *Kpakpa Désenchanté*)

TUNISIA

Jaouhari Sahnoun, a reporter for the banned al-Nahda party newspaper *al-Fajr,* died in a

Tunis hospital on 25 January. He had been in detention since March 1991 and was serving a 15-year sentence for 'attempting to overthrow the government'. (PEN)

Kamel Labidi, previously with the official news agency Tunis Africa Presse (TAP) and correspondent with French daily *La Croix* since 1988, was denied press accreditation in February. He was dismissed by TAP in March 1994 for 'professional misconduct' after his interview with the former president of the Tunisian League for Human Rights was published in *La Croix*. (RSF)

Jalel Maalej, a Tunisian academic resident in Paris, who was arrested on 4 December on returning to Tunisia and held incommunicado for a month, was sentenced on 8 February to three years in prison for belonging to al-Nahda. (AI)

Mohamed Kilani, a leading member of the unauthorised Tunisian Workers' Communist Party (PCOT), was sentenced to two years' imprisonment on 22 February for supporting an unauthorised organisation and holding meetings without permission. (AI)

TURKEY

On 28 December Ocak Isik Yutcu, the first editor-in-chief of the now defunct *Özgür Gündem*, was sentenced to 25 years in prison for 'separatist' articles published in the pro-Kurdish daily in 1991. (CPJ)

In a police operation on 4

January, 30 suspected members of the banned Turkish Revolutionary Communist Party (TDKP) were detained in Istanbul, among them Zöhre Aksoy, Tacsim Şimşek, Mürüvvet Günel, Şükrü Taş, Kiraz Özcan, Emine Akcan, Ahmet Mete Kekec, Hüseyin Toprak and Reşit Güleryüz. Five of the detainees — Hüseyin Aksoy, Kemal Yadirgi, Seyda Gül, Hüseyin Demirli and Ismet Dursun — were formally arrested on 13 January. (AI)

On 6 January police began to seize copies of the pro-Kurdish daily *Özgür Ülke* before it went to final press, marking articles that violated the Anti-Terror Law. The newspaper was obliged to remove the articles before reprinting a second time for distribution. The paper's 18 January edition appeared with two blank pages owing to prior censorship. Editions of the right-wing weekly *Taraf*, the left-wing weeklies *Gercek* and *Alinteri*, and the pro-Kurdish weekly *Newroz* also suffered similar vetting in January. (AI, Reuter, RSF)

On 13 January Ali Baransel, head of the radio and television high council, warned broadcasters who transmit 'separatist propaganda' that they are being closely watched and risk being closed down. (SWB)

Özgür Ülke reporters Hüsnü Akgül and Hidayet Pehlivan were detained on 16 January but released on 18 January. Ismail Hakki Keleci, who was detained on 19 January,

remains in detention. (AI)

Yaşar Kemal (*Index* 1/1995, p141) is to be prosecuted under article 8 of the Anti-Terror Law, which forbids 'propaganda damaging state unity'. The charge, brought on 23 January, relates to an article he wrote for *Der Spiegel* on 10 January. (Reuter, PEN)

On 24 January the Van office of *Özgür Ülke* was raided by plainclothes police. One of the correspondents, Dogan Denizhan, was detained and released three days later. Salih Guher (*Index* 1/1995) was also released on 30 January after more than three weeks in custody. (AI)

On 3 February *Özgür Ülke* was banned from publication after a court ruled that it was a successor to *Özgür Gündem*, which was closed down in 1994, and therefore subject to the same ban. On 6 February two further publications were banned: the left-wing *Kurtulus* was found to be a successor to *Mucadele* magazine, banned in October 1994; and *Dengè-Azadi,* a follow-on from *Azadi*, which was outlawed in May 1994. (CPJ)

The editor of the weekly *Alinteri*, Saliha Yaptaterek, was arrested on 9 February. On the same day the paper's Adana and Antakya offices were raided by police who also confiscated papers. On 20 February the paper was banned for one month for 'separatism'. (CPJ, *Alinteri*)

On 13 February Mahmut Şakar, Nimetullah Gündüz,

Abdullah Çağer and Melinke Alp (*Index* 1/1995) of the Diyarbakir branch of the Human Rights Association (IHD) were remanded in custody until 17 April. Five further members of the branch — Sinan Tanrikulu, Firat Anli, Hanifi Işik, Şerit Atmaça and Servet Ayhan — were detained in a police raid on 27 February, along with Ioannis Kokkindhis, a journalist with the Greek paper *Adhesmevtos Tipos*, and his interpreter Michail Girmis. (AI, SWB, Journalists' Safety Service)

Recent publications: *Advocacy and the Rule of Law in Turkey: Advocates Under Attack* (Bar Human Rights Committee, January 1995, 92pp); *A Policy of Denial* (AI, February 1995, 36pp)

UKRAINE

Over 500 members of left-wing parties and organisations demonstrated in front of the State Committee for Radio and Television Broadcasting in Kiev on 22 February, alleging political censorship and demanding equal airtime for their organisations. (OMRI, SWB)

Recent publication: *The 1994 Parliamentary and Presidential Elections: Monitoring of the Election Coverage in the Ukrainian Mass Media, Final Report* (European Institute for the Media, October 1994, 231pp)

UNITED ARAB EMIRATES

Sheikh Al-Ali, author of a number of books on Islamic law, was detained on 16 January by police who searched his home and seized several books. It is unclear whether he was detained because of his views on Islam, or for his criticism of the government. (PEN)

UNITED KINGDOM

On 11 January Alexander Malikov, a correspondent for the Russian television station Ostankino, was expelled for 'reasons of national security'. (*Financial Times*, SWB)

Tarsem Singh Purewal, editor of Britain's biggest Punjabi newspaper, *Des Pardes*, was shot dead on 24 January near his office in Southall, London. Police believe his death may be connected to articles he published that were sympathetic to the idea of a separate Sikh state of Khalistan. (*Times*)

On 1 February the government dismissed allegations that Iranian or Syrian groups had been involved in the Lockerbie bombing. Foreign secretary Douglas Hurd reaffirmed that Libya alone was responsible, despite a leaked document from US Intelligence which implicated a senior Iranian minister. (*Guardian*)

An appeals court ruled on 3 February that illegal immigrants seeking political asylum must stay in prison while their cases are considered. Approximately 650 asylum seekers are currently being held in British jails awaiting a ruling. The case will now be taken to the House of Lords. (Reuter)

The governing Conservative Party followed through its threat to close down the satirical magazine *Scallywag* on 18 February by issuing libel writs against nine companies that distribute the magazine. An article in the January issue alleged that the Conservatives were planning a 'dirty tricks' campaign against the opposition Labour Party. (*Independent*)

On 20 February it was alleged that Kamlesh Bahl, the head of the Equal Opportunities Commission, had delayed publication of a report that showed the detrimental effects of Conservative policies on women workers. Bahl is a former Conservative activist and personal appointee of the prime minister (*Independent*)

Royal Ulster Constabulary officers raided the Sinn Féin office in Derry on 20 February, following the most serious anti-RUC protest in the city for several years. Two Sinn Féin delegates to the Forum for Peace and Reconciliation, Mary Nelis and Dodie McGuinness, were arrested and taken to Castlereagh interrogation centre in Belfast. (Irish press)

On 24 February the hearing of an action brought against publishers Savoy Books for breach of the Obscene Publications Act began in Manchester. Over 4,000 comic books were seized by police because of their alleged racist content. Many also contained a satirical portrayal of James Anderton, the former chief constable of Manchester. If the action is successful the comics could be destroyed. (Savoy Books)

Kani Yilmaz, the European representative of the Kurdistan Workers' Party (PKK), continues to be held in solitary confinement in Belmarch prison. His extradition hearing, due to start in February, has been postponed until the first week of May. (Kurdistan Information Centre)

USA

In autumn 1994 Andrew Archambeau was charged under Michigan's anti-stalking law for stalking a woman via electronic mail and her telephone answering machine; apparently he did not approach her in person. Michigan is the only state to include electronic communications in its stalking law. (*New York Times*)

After months of angry criticism of a proposed exhibition about the dropping of the atomic bomb on Hiroshima, the Smithsonian Institution decided in January to eliminate text and pictures of the Japanese victims and to display only the fuselage of the Enola Gay (the aeroplane that dropped the bomb), a plaque and a film of the plane's crew (*Index* 6/1994). (Reuter)

Legislation that would make all telecommunications providers doing business in the USA legally responsible for everything sent over their networks was introduced to a Senate subcommittee this winter. The Communications Decency Act of 1995 (S 314) is aimed at curbing obscene material in cyberspace and would impose large fines and jail sentences on businesses, such as electronic bulletin boards, where the prohibited speech appeared. It would also force operators of electronic networks to monitor in advance all messages sent over them. The limits of speech in cyberspace came under further scrutiny in February, when a University of Michigan college student, Jake A Baker, was charged with interstate transmission of a threat after he posted a story on the Internet about torturing, raping and murdering a fellow student, whom he named. (National Writers Union, Electronic Messaging Association)

On 17 January, the Supreme Court declined to hear an appeal from Stephen Knox, who was convicted of pornography in 1991 for possessing videotapes of young girls in suggestive poses, though they were not undressed. The decision leaves intact a lower court's ruling that neither nudity nor pictures of genitals are required for a child pornography conviction (*Index* 4&5/1994). (Knight Ridder)

In February the Electronic Frontier Foundation sponsored a lawsuit by Daniel J Bernstein, a graduate student at the University of California, against the State Department in an effort to ease non-governmental development of encryption technology (*Index* 1&2/1994). Bernstein claims that government regulations interfere with his First Amendment rights by preventing him from posting his encryption programme, called Snuffle, on the Internet. (*Boston Globe*)

The National Endowments for the Arts and Humanities and the Corporation for Public Broadcasting (CPB) — the primary federal agencies for funding culture in the country — came under attack in Congress in February. A House subcommittee has recommended cuts of $5 million for each of the Endowments for the next fiscal year. CPB would be cut by 15 per cent in 1996 and a further 30 per cent in 1997. (National Campaign for Freedom of Expression, *Boston Globe*)

On 21 February, the Supreme Court decided that Amtrak is part of the government and can be sued for violation of civil rights, clearing the way for a lawsuit brought by artist Michael Lebron, whose commissioned artwork at Penn Station, New York was deemed too 'political' (*Index* 1/1995). (*Washington Post*)

Legislation making English the national language and stopping all federal bilingual programs was introduced in Congress on 21 February. (Associated Press)

On 22 February, the Supreme Court overturned a 1989 law that barred approximately 1.7 million employees of the federal government from collecting honoraria for speeches and articles on subjects unrelated to their work. Fees for speaking or writing on subjects linked to official duties or agency business are still prohibited. (Associated Press)

On 28 February a code banning hate speech at Stanford University in California was ruled unconstitutional because it was excessively broad and banned only words based on sex and race. (Associated Press)

On 1 March, the Supreme Court heard arguments on whether the University of Virginia violated the rights of a student when it refused to fund a religious publication. The case pits the First Amendment separation of church and state against the First Amendment guarantees of free speech and free press. A decision is due by June. (Reuter)

Recent publications: *Defending Pornography*, by Nadine Strossen (Scribner, 1995); *Hate Speech: The History of an American Controversy*, by Samuel Walker (Univ of Nebraska Press, 1994); *On the Front Line: Law Enforcement Views on the Death Penalty* (Death Penalty Information Center, February 1995, 25pp)

VIETNAM

The government lifted a five-week ban on the weekly paper *The Hanoian* on 25 February. The paper had been suspended over a critical article on the state's prohibition of fireworks, introduced after 71 people died during last year's Tet festivities. The Ministry of Information and Culture said the article violated the press law and that the 'editor, editorial board and article's author were severely reprimanded'. *The Hanoian*, like all other Vietnamese newspapers, is state owned. (Reuter)

ZAMBIA

On 8 December 1994, armed police raided the editorial offices of the *Post* newspaper, with warrants to search for 'seditious and defamatory material'. The *Post* claimed the police were looking for a 'compromising' picture of President Chiluba. (*News from Zambia*)

President Chiluba has approved the Parliamentary and Ministerial Code of Conduct Act, which includes a provision for jailing anyone found guilty of making a false allegation against a political leader. (*News from Zambia*) ❏

Compiled by: Anna Feldman, Jason Garner, Oren Gruenbaum (Africa); Nan Levinson, Lesley McCave, Nathalie Vartanpour-Naalbandian (Americas); Nicholas McAulay, Atanu Roy, Jason Stephens (Asia); Colin Isham (central Asia); Laura Bruni, Robin Jones, Vera Rich (eastern Europe and CIS); Jamie McLeish, Philippa Nugent (Middle East); Daniel Brett, Robert Maharajh (western Europe) ❏

BRITO

RSF

Contributors

Mumia Abu-Jamal is an award-winning print and radio journalist. Despite convincing evidence of his innocence, he has spent the last 13 years on Pennsylvania's death row; an 'expedited' date for his execution is feared shortly; **Gerry Adams** is president of Sinn Féin, Northern Ireland; **Hugo Bedau** is Austin Fletcher professor of philosophy and director, Center for the Study of Decision Making at Tufts University, Massachusetts. This paper is taken from a lecture at the Centre for Capital Punishment Studies, School of Law, University of Westminster (London) where he was a visiting professor; **Beatrix Campbell** is a journalist; her most recent book is *Goliath: Britain's Dangerous Places* (Methuen, 1993). **Alan Clark** was Conservative MP for Plymouth (Sutton) 1974-1992. He served in the ministries of trade and defence, and is a member of the Privy Council. His controversial *Diaries* was published in 1993; **Ellie Cronin** and **Akter Hussein** are pupils at Islington Green School, London; **Richard Dieter** is executive director of the Death Penalty Information Center, Washington, DC; **Bassem Eïd** is a fieldworker with B'Tselem, a Jerusalem-based human rights organisation; **Penelope Farmer's** most recent novel is *Snakes and Ladders* (Little Brown/Abacus, London, 1993); **Mark Fisher** is Labour MP for Stoke-on-Trent Central. He unsuccessfully introduced the Right to Know Bill in the House of Commons in 1993; **Paul Foot** writes for *Private Eye* and the *Guardian;* **Maurice Frankel** is director of the London-based Campaign for Freedom of Information; **Charles Glass** is the author of *Tribes with Flags* and *Money for Old Rope*, both published by Picador; **Teresa Hayter** is a member of the Campaign to Close Campsfield; **Christopher Hird** produces TV documentaries. His *Murdoch, the Great Escape*, was published by Warner in 1991; **Christopher Hitchens** writes for the *Nation* and *Vanity Fair;* **Godfrey Hodgson** is director of the Reuter Foundation Programme, Oxford; **Matthew Hoffman** is an editor at the *Independent*, London; **Gitobu Imanyara** is a lawyer and editor-in-chief of the *Nairobi Law Monthly*, Kenya; **Helena Kennedy** chairs the London-based Charter 88 Council; **Saul Lehrfreund** is a human rights executive at the London law firm, Simons Muirhead & Burton; the Malawian poet **Jack Mapanje** currently teaches creative writing at Leeds University. His latest book of poems is *The Chattering Wagtails of Mikuyu Prison* (Heinemann, Oxford, 1993); **Cecile Marcel** is working at Article 19, London; **Caroline Moorehead** is a writer and film maker specialising in human rights; **Aryeh Neier** is president of the Open Society Institute, New York; **Julian Petley** is head of Communication and Information Studies at Brunel University, UK; **Andrew Puddephatt** is general secretary of Liberty (National Council for Civil Liberties), UK; **Ghazi Rabihavi** is an Iranian novelist now in London, most of whose work remains with the censor's office in Iran; **Michael L Radelet** is professor of sociology, University of Florida. This paper was written while the author was a visiting professor at the Centre for Capital Punishment Studies, University of Westminster; **Vera Rich** is a specialist in Belarusian and Ukrainian matters; **James D Ross** is based in Phnom Penh with the International Human Rights Law Group; **Alexander Solzhenitsyn**, Russia's Nobel Prize-winning author of the *Gulag Archipelago* and the *First Circle*, returned to Russia in 1994; **Davrell Tien** is a freelance journalist based in Sweden; **Martin Tystad** is a Norwegian journalist visiting *Index;* **Cecilia Valenzuela,** a Peruvian journalist, writes for *Caretas* magazine, Lima; and **Judith Vidal-Hall** visited Baku with the aid agency Caritas, Denmark ❏